The M
Syndrome

The Mandarin Syndrome

The Secret Life of Senior Bureaucrats

Maurice Henrie

Translated from the French
by David Homel and Wayne Grady

University of Ottawa Press
Ottawa • London • Paris

© University of Ottawa Press, 1990
ISBN 0-7766-0294-2
Printed and bound in Canada

Canadian Cataloguing in Publication Data
Henrie, Maurice, 1936-

The mandarin syndrome: the secret life of senior
bureaucrats

Translation of: La vie secrète des grands
bureaucrates.
ISBN 0-7766-0294-2

1. Government executives—Anecdotes.
2. Government executives—Humor. I. Title.

HD38.4.H4613 1990   351.007'4'0207   C90-090492-5

UNIVERSITÉ   UNIVERSITY
D'OTTAWA   OF OTTAWA

Design: Judith Gregory

The masculine pronoun has been used in a generic
sense throughout this book.

To all bureaucrats—junior and senior, men and women, federal, provincial and municipal— including those in the private sector and in international organizations.

Now he could see the Castle above him, clearly
defined in the glittering air.

Franz Kafka, *The Castle*

Contents

Preface

I would not write a book that was simply humorous. So the humour in this one is merely a pretext, a lure intended to attract and hold attention, in the hope that the reader will go on reading and, ideally, think more and more and laugh less and less. I do not know of any other way to arouse interest in a subject which is considered by most people to be extremely boring.

But there is a catch. I made no attempt to separate humour from seriousness, fiction from reality, truth from invention. I left this to the reader. And my experience in this regard is that the reader does it very well and with an astonishing ease. Perhaps there is an instinctive understanding that these are more than Newfie jokes and that the reader is expected to participate in taking what is written and extracting its essence. He or she therefore co-operates willingly, I have found, and without hesitation.

Density, however, may be a problem. Few people will be inclined to read a large number of pages without feeling the need to pause for a while and come back later. This is appropriate and advisable. In fact, given the structure of this book — because it is highly structured, in spite of appearances — it is relatively easy to stop reading at almost any point without affecting understanding to any degree.

It is true that reality is somewhat distorted here, that things cannot always be that dark. I agree. Nonetheless, the substance of this book was drawn directly from reality, that is, from the actual observation of senior bureaucrats over a period of more than twenty years. It was obviously a conscious choice to present only the aspect of this reality that best supported the overall thrust of what I was trying to show. I leave to another bureaucrat the task of writing a book to show the other side of the coin. But it may be some time before it is available and one wonders whether it will be worth waiting for.

Finally, I have no hope, no illusion, that bureaucracies will somehow be improved, let alone changed to any degree, by my effort. They will go on pursuing their own course in history (even though they will never be part of it). But to effect change was not my purpose. I will be content if I can bring a smile to a reader's face, if I can get from him or her even a slight nod of recognition.

1
Merit

He has graduated from university, but just barely. He missed the Honours degree he had coveted; he did not get the woman he had hoped to marry, nor the position he had been eyeing in a certain commercial institution. He has failed to become a candidate in municipal politics. He has, accordingly, changed his plans. He has become a public servant, eventually a senior bureaucrat, having entered one of those rare careers in which real worth is not considered indispensable, and in fact is often set aside in favour of other, more humane, more civilized, more . . . personal considerations.

∞ ∞ ∞

Silence and solemnity in a mandarin is often a form of fraud. For in remaining quiet, by adopting a sober mien, the senior bureaucrat lays claim to a depth, a weightiness, an equilibrium, that do not in fact belong to him. So long as he keeps his mouth shut the fiction is maintained, and the magic works in his favour. Let him but speak and he breaks the spell with his very first words. Where one had expected to hear the roaring of a lion, one hears only the braying of an ass.

∞ ∞ ∞

Self-interest, the anticipation of personal gain or perhaps even true dedication, can raise the senior public servant — who

owes his position, after all, not to competence but to favouritism
— to hitherto unsuspected heights of cleverness, at times even
brilliance. Such buoyancy, however, is invariably short-lived,
and the senior bureaucrat soon sinks back to his more accustomed state, like a muscle after orgasm. There is no lasting effect
in his routine: Dullness is returned to its rightful throne, and
Folly resumes its momentarily interrupted reign.

∞ ∞ ∞

The senior bureaucrat puts in place a set of criteria whose
purpose is to eliminate undesirable candidates for employment,
especially undesirables with merit, which are the most dangerous kind. Without such criteria, it would be difficult to find acceptable reasons for blocking the advance of a candidate who
has merit but who, for one reason or another, is not the choice
of the mandarin.

∞ ∞ ∞

In order to become a senior bureaucrat, it is first necessary
to act as if you already were one. It is wonderful how many people will be taken in by so simple a stratagem — so many that it
will soon be believed that you actually occupy the position you
are pretending to hold. And when everyone around you believes
you to be a senior bureaucrat, you will end up believing it yourself. From there, it is but a simple step to actually becoming one.
No one resembles a senior bureaucrat more than he who is about
to be made one.

∞ ∞ ∞

Never express gratitude to a senior bureaucrat. In his heart,
he knows he does not deserve it.

∞ ∞ ∞

Narrow-mindedness in certain senior bureaucrats is peculiar
to them, and must not be interpreted in its usual sense as a de-

ficiency of intellect, an excessive moral severity, evidence of a strictly literal and mean-spirited apprehension of reality, or even an unnatural resistance to new ideas . . .

No, none of those things come into play here. It is not so much narrow-mindedness as a genuine narrowness of mind, a kind of cerebral bottleneck through which new ideas may enter not in lumps but only in single file. Their brains are incapable of grasping several concepts at once, at least not with any sort of effectiveness, nor can they deal with more than one task at a time. They are like computers with very weak memories; they will eventually respond to a command, but only if you give them enough time.

∞ ∞ ∞

According to the merit principle, all public servants have an equal opportunity of rising to the top of the bureaucratic pyramid. It's just that some are quietly invited to step into the elevator, while the rest are noisily herded onto the staircase.

∞ ∞ ∞

Let us suppose there is a post to be filled. The senior bureaucrat instinctively eschews the normal, long-established codes of procedure, the boring old criteria, the inflexible standards, the basic ground rules, the whole administrative mumbo-jumbo that serves no other purpose than to curtail his field of action, to limit his ability to come to his own arbitrary but inspired decisions. Who needs all these curricula vitae, these testaments to superior productivity, these calculations of seniority, these lists of positions held and university degrees attained, these formulaic letters of recommendation from perfect strangers . . .?

The mandarin prefers a more flexible, a more personal, a more humane approach. He makes discreet enquiries into the candidate's family background, where he was born, what schools he attended and with whom. He tries to find out who the candidate's friends are, and asks them for comments and recommendations. He mentions the candidate's name to his own secretary, to see if she has heard anything about him that isn't generally known. If possible, he points the candidate out on the street to one of his colleagues. He tries to pick up any gossip that's going the rounds. He assesses whether the newcomer has the right chemistry to fit into his organization. He may even go so far as to invite the candidate to lunch — as a kind of cover-up for an initial sounding-out — at which it will be discovered that they both share an absolute passion for sailing. He satisfies himself that the candidate attaches no undue importance to any old list of academic accomplishments. He takes account of physical qualities, especially if the candidate is female. Dependability, discretion, the ability to appreciate from the subtlest of hints the delicacy, complexity and danger inherent in certain situations — those are the traits he admires. He tries to gauge the amount of empathy the subordinate-to-be inspires in him. Then, by way of cementing his appreciation, he recalls the glowing words spoken with a strange insistence by the Deputy Minister himself with regard to this particular candidate; and he remembers that he owes a favour to such-and-such a colleague who, for obscure but no doubt very good reasons, supports the applicant's candidacy; finally, he takes into consideration the fact — discovered through one of his private investigations — that the future employee is also a distant cousin of the Minister's, though luckily he doesn't have the same last name.

Only then, when his decision has been definitely and for all practical purposes reached, does the senior bureaucrat announce that there will be a competition for the post. First he sees to it that the number of applicants will be as low as possible; he gives an early deadline for submissions, and limits the geographical area and population base from which all candidates must be drawn. He then arranges a series of interviews (which will require most of the candidates to come from great distances by airplane at the taxpayers' expense) for all those who made it onto the "shortlist," which was quite objectively compiled by eliminating all applicants who had not taken a course in Sanskrit given in German by either a Swedish or Finnish professor with one leg at the University of California at Berkeley.

The final step in his strategy is to ask a few of the more conciliatory, understanding mandarins among his acquaintances to join him in making up a selection committee that will have surprisingly little difficulty in unanimously endorsing his own point of view.

∞ ∞ ∞

In the mind of the senior bureaucrat, merit consists of the following components, in varying proportions and in no particular order: friendliness, charisma, influence and family connections. This is by no means an exhaustive list, but it contains the four principal ingredients. What is left out is negligible, and tends toward poetry.

∞ ∞ ∞

True merit is not determined by the candidate's value, but by the judge's perception, and is a function of time and space. Change the judge, the hour or the location, and you would have a totally different winner. We recognize merit when we see it because we are the judges, say all senior mandarins.

∞ ∞ ∞

The sharpest thorn in the side of the senior bureaucrat is the knowledge that he owes his position to pure chance, and not to his own merit. How delightful it would be to believe that there existed some link, however tenuous, between his position and his own ability to fill it.

∞ ∞ ∞

The senior bureaucrat goes to cocktail parties in order to find out who is on the verge of losing his reputation and who is about to gain one, whose career is winding down and whose is gaining momentum. Nothing in the world is more dangerous to him than not knowing which of his colleagues to cut, and which to cultivate. Like a wolf, his muzzle in the air to sniff which way the wind is blowing, the senior bureaucrat senses the birth and circulation of such information, and adjusts his behaviour accordingly.

Genius and the senior bureaucrat: two naturally incompatible and mutually exclusive notions . . . even for the senior bureaucrat himself.

∞ ∞ ∞

The senior bureaucrat must be constantly on guard against too much merit. An employee who has it could easily become a divisive factor, leading to discord and disequilibrium within the section. Similarly, the senior bureaucrat does not want to be given an umbrella too big to fit into his briefcase. Nor does he want speeches made about him, however flattering they may be, that would be more appropriate to a Minister or a President than to himself. A moderate competence is infinitely preferable to excessive talent in the eyes of a senior public servant, whose highest goal is the uniform and harmonious operation of his section.

∞ ∞ ∞

There are senior bureaucrats who are so lazy that they spend hours on end in their offices doing nothing, neither for the government nor for themselves; whose sole aim in life is to savour the sweet sensation of doing absolutely nothing at all.

∞ ∞ ∞

It is a good idea to hang photographs of mandarins in the offices and along the corridors of government buildings. Otherwise, who on earth would remember them? And what on earth for?

∞ ∞ ∞

When the son of a senior bureaucrat follows in his father's footsteps, the very fact that his name is known in the department opens certain doors for him that otherwise would remain closed for quite a long time. He thus gains years on those of his colleagues who have run-of-the-mill names, and who therefore must travel the same road under their own steam.

Some senior bureaucrats are like Blue Point Siamese cats: they have been tamed, and fed, and pampered; they yawn and stretch before the radiator; they doze on salmon-pink velour cushions. Set them outside on a cool fall night, and they would die of hunger, exposure and loneliness.

∞ ∞ ∞

The top bureaucracy is like a failed experiment that no one has bothered to write up.

∞ ∞ ∞

When a senior bureaucrat makes a grand gesture, performs a gratuitous act of kindness, or accomplishes a brilliant feat, one is once again dazzled by the mysterious and unpredictable mechanisms of pure chance.

∞ ∞ ∞

Like the intangible odour of steaks wafting from the sun-drenched patios of the capital on any given summer Sunday afternoon, rumours drift through the air of the senior bureaucrats' city and form a magnetic and invisible fluid mass in which a hundred different anecdotes are continuously being disassembled, reassembled, shuffled together and infinitesimally altered with each successive repetition: indiscretions whispered with pleasure and precision to a breathless listener; malicious stories invented on the spot and swallowed whole; witty slanders sprinkled with venomous defamations; raw truths tempered with plausible explanations, probable interpretations and creditable excuses; lies so well told they assume the cloak of gospel and cast doubt upon truth itself; reports deliberately unverified lest their realities be much less spicy and original than their tellings; honest declarations tarted up with humorous exaggerations; blatant falsehoods robbed of their ability to shock by falling on such eager ears; approximations that mimic exactitude to perfection; betrayals that are parodies of sympathy and compassion.

All of this is jumbled together in the huge, broiling cauldron that is the Public Service, where it becomes an over-cooked stew in which the individual flavour of each ingredient is completely lost, resulting in a formless, colourless, odourless and tasteless paste. But make no mistake; you are dealing here with fundamental matter, whose function is to determine the reputation and career of all who pass through it. The overall perception of each person — who is friend, who is foe — is determined by it. This basic substance is the ultimate source of every opinion collectively shared by every mandarin. The process is cyclical, and can take years to complete.

"But," say the senior bureaucrats, "it is this very slowness that guarantees the correctness of the diagnosis. It eliminates the need for juries, interviews, examinations, probationary periods, work-level assessments, the whole cumbersome machinery that can only be a partial reflection of reality at best. In the end, all these methods, these 'objective criteria,' are useless. They were invented by idealistic dreamers, by intellectuals whose sole passion is for exactitude and absolute fairness — in short, by innocents who will never become senior bureaucrats themselves. They are undertaking the idiotic task of trying to measure, objectively and scientifically, a complex series of infinitely variable phenomena. No, our method is much better, based as it is on instinct, the gradual accumulation of subtle impressions, and an infinitely elongated series of very small judgements.

"You say that gossip is the source of all human misery? Well, you are entitled to your opinion. Laugh at our methods if you wish. Keep your philosophical pretentions if they amuse you. But you will find that everything passes through the rumour-mill in the end. Ours is a mill that grinds slowly, my friend, but exceeding fine. Its inexorable process is at work at this very moment, even as we speak, delivering its weighty judgement on everyone, including yourself. A judgement against which there is no appeal."

∞ ∞ ∞

Next to the molehill of political patronage there is the mountain of bureaucratic favouritism, the summit of which is totally obscured by clouds. While journalists scamper around trying to track down clear-cut cases of backroom influence-peddling among our elected officials, senior mandarins, dressed in their long, black robes, are busy handing out patronage appointments on an unimaginable scale — silently, discreetly, prudently masking their activities behind a barrage of logical, reasonable explanations that can be delivered at a moment's notice when required. Which, given the lily-white reputations they are so careful to cultivate, is never.

∞ ∞ ∞

It is very rare for a senior bureaucrat to allow the demands of the merit principle to take precedence over his own will, or to thwart his own desires. In fact, if such a confrontation even arises, it means something in the system has broken down. Under normal circumstances, there exists only a seamless harmony between the desires of the senior bureaucrat and the merit principle as it is understood by those who work under the senior bureaucrat. That is, by those who wish to keep their jobs, or avoid being silenced, or to be highly recommended, or perhaps even promoted.

∞ ∞ ∞

A senior bureaucrat considers it a sign of bad taste — or at least of bad judgement — if he takes under his wing an employee who has been made available ("fired" is such an ugly, final word) by another senior bureaucrat. These things have been stringently codified, you understand; tradition is a tyrant, and team spirit is a hard task-master. Solidarity forever, and all that. A senior bureaucrat who shows even a modicum of sympathy toward, pity for, or commiseration with the victim, runs the risk of being branded a traitor, or a loner, or — worst of all — out of touch. Not to mention that providing the victim with a refuge, however temporary, could be interpreted by those higher up as an aspersion cast upon the judgement of a fellow senior public servant, the one who had let the victim go in the first place ("dismissed" is such an old-fashioned, snobbish word). It is to imply that one's colleague has stuffed something useful, recuperable, recyclable down the old departmental rat-hole. What is more, one's own judgement, one's very instinct for survival, is likely to be called into question if one is seen to have tried to put to use an item already declared redundant ("terminated" sounds so brutal . . .) and beyond redemption. Whether or not the employee in question is guilty or has been made a scapegoat is a matter of supreme insignificance, since not only has his sentence been pronounced, but his execution has already taken place.

Thus the senior bureaucrat watches with an unflinching dispassion as the unfortunate wretch, desperately trying to stave off the inevitable, goes through his slow death-agony, which can last for months on end — following up circuitous leads that go nowhere, knocking on doors that never open — in the vain hope of selling his services at however derisory a price. No one wants him. He is a rapidly falling body, subject to the law of physics which states that the longer his fall takes, the more it accelerates. Until finally he is falling so fast that he is little more than a blur in the corner of one's eye, heading toward the door.

∞ ∞ ∞

Being in the company of a senior bureaucrat can be a lively and invigorating experience — it makes one feel good about oneself.

∞ ∞ ∞

Senior bureaucrats may be divided into two distinct categories: those who have more merit than they have had promotions; and those who have had more promotions than they have merit. The first are more numerous, but the second are happier.

∞ ∞ ∞

American customs are often strange and sometimes surprising, don't you find? Take their elections, for example. Or rather, the period immediately following their elections. Each time, the top bureaucrats in the country, those who occupy the highest levels in the administrative pyramid, are summarily replaced by another set of top bureaucrats appointed by the newly elected government. Vague official explanations would have it that the new set are more in tune with the new Administration, that they are more readily disposed to carry out the policies and directives of the new regime, that they are better able to put into place programs that accurately reflect the true intentions of the government of the day. That, at least, is the theory, and it looks fairly convincing on paper. In reality, however, the practice opens the door to a good dose of what we in this country call political patronage. Down there, though, the thing is accomplished so openly, so candidly, so equally by Republicans and Democrats alike, that it has acquired a kind of legitimacy, even respectability, and it never occurs to anyone to be scandalized by it. As is well known, the best way to defuse criticism is not to hide anything that may lend itself to controversy or that can be judged reprehensible.

How different things are here at home. How much purer. Atop even the least significant of public buildings in Canada there flies the triumvirate of standards signifying Democracy, Justice and Merit. Unlike the Americans, we in Canada make every effort to avoid tainting our elections with what can only be described as a blood-bath — the sudden and rapid replacement of one batch of senior bureaucrats with a fresh lot. On this soil, in which human rights have so noisily flourished, public executions are considered to be in very bad form. Better to do it behind closed doors. Where the noise won't disturb the popularity of the new government which would naturally sweep all political considerations aside in order to help the underdog, and for whom the art of governing consists above all in the science of staying in power.

Therefore not only are our senior public servants left in place, but also our second-, third- and fourth-ranked bureaucrats, those who, having been installed, coddled and cuddled by the former government, are now waiting in line, one behind the other, for someone ahead of them to die of a heart attack, fall out of favour, or otherwise disappear from the face of the earth. Still, these professional profiteers know perfectly well that, despite the present government's public display of confidence, which is a kind of provisional cease-fire, despite the apparent security of their position, their days are nonetheless numbered. They are intensely aware that the crossed threads of a high-powered, precision telescope mounted on a high-calibre Weatherby rifle are trained calmly and steadily on their perspiring foreheads. They wait only for the sudden disappearance of the parquet beneath their feet; their nostrils smell nothing but gunpowder; walking home late at night, they turn around at every corner to see who is standing in the shadows behind them, silently watching. Their anxiety is increased, if that were possible, when, after a few weeks, maybe a few months, one of their protectors higher up — a distant relation, or a guardian angel — suddenly falls from grace and, without fanfare, without even a farewell, is gone. They cross their arms and stare silently at their reflection in the office window, they wait — forever — without moving, without daring to think, as if for something dreadful that seems imminent but which, in the end, might not happen at all. Who knows who the next victim will be? Or from what height he will fall? A supervisor? A section head? And will he drag others down too, those lesser beings who, in happier times, had clung to him like parasites?

Very soon, panic sets in. They begin to look around for ways to disassociate themselves from anything to do with the former government. Like defeated soldiers stranded in enemy territory, they change uniforms, avoid certain sectors, learn the language and customs of their new country, hide their old accents. And all for nothing. Even as the newly elected Cabinet Ministers are smiling their assurances, the most important departmental heads are rolling off the guillotine, and new heads are taking their place, and those heads are pushing other heads under the blade, and slowly, inexorably, the chopping gains momentum.

There is no escape. What began as a political process quickly becomes a bureaucratic one, and the press doesn't bother with bureaucratic processes. The public remains blissfully unaware that anything is happening. Ministers and their coterie never dirty their own hands — they hire senior bureaucrats to do their work for them, someone dispensable, someone specially trained in the art of termination, someone who wields the axe so well that the victims hardly feel anything at all. There are senior bureaucrats who do nothing else but go around dismantling departments, one after another, for their entire career. They come and go, turn up here and there, making no sound except for the occasional "thwunk" when their knife finds a soft body, an organ, a living target. The true public servants, the "lifers," those who do their work and keep their heads down and haven't the slightest inclination toward power, watch this secret process of purification helplessly. They shake their heads. They are glad they have never risen so high that they have to be brought so low.

After a while, the purge loses momentum and eventually stops altogether, usually for lack of victims. In a year, two years at most, when the dust has settled, there is no sign of disorder, no trace of battle, no bloodstains on the carpet. On the contrary, there is nothing to see but fresh, smiling, confident faces. New faces, admittedly, and it may take a while to get to know them. But there is plenty of time — two, maybe three years, until the next election. Then the whole thing will start up again, the smiling denials, the invocations to the great God of Merit, the assurances to all and sundry that everything is just fine, thank you, the dropping of the bodies over the cliffs.

No sir, those Americans do things differently from us, no doubt about it. Especially in the spheres of culture and politics. We must resist their influence at all costs. We must maintain those traditional values that make us unique. We must preserve our national heritage.

∞ ∞ ∞

In most people, silence and economy of expression are signs of wisdom and experience. In senior bureaucrats, they are more often the result of ignorance.

∞ ∞ ∞

Ever since he read somewhere that the Emperor Caligula wanted to have his horse, Incitatus, installed as a senator, the senior bureaucrat has had trouble sleeping. He has a recurring nightmare, in which he and his colleagues have been replaced by a whole stableful of horses, and no one has noticed the difference.

Luck is the most unsettling word in the senior bureaucrat's lexicon. Every time he hears it applied to himself, he feels his own sense of personal worth being raked over the coals, to be superseded by the notion of mere chance. Luck suppresses, or at least diminishes, every reason he has ever invented for feeling proud of himself. It destroys the illusion that he genuinely deserves whatever it is he has, or is. It exposes him to those sharp pangs of doubt that, like herpes, may sometimes go into remission, but will never, ever go away.

∞ ∞ ∞

The senior-bureaucrat-to-be will do anything in his power to rise to the top; he will employ any means, use any method or any person, or pay any price, so long as he reaches his goal. Once he has attained it, though, he will immediately let it be known that it was his own personal merit that got him there, and not a favourable combination of circumstances, patronage, ass-kissing, string-pulling and file-fixing. Like the survivor of a shipwreck trying to erase from his memory all those hands gripping the sides of the lifeboat, threatening to tip it over, that he had to chop off with an axe, the mandarin is haunted by a detestable past that, for the sake of his own sanity, he must try to blot out. All the honours, the fine reputation, the respect of his peers and the esteem of his betters, all that counts for nothing if he cannot believe that he has risen to where he is through innate talent, hard work, clean living and intrinsic merit.

∞ ∞ ∞

Those who hold the merit principle in the greatest contempt are those whose job it is to apply it. Who better knows the difficulty, if not the impossibility, of administering a notion that is not only abstract to begin with, but is also repeatedly subject to subtle and usually anonymous pressures from above and even from outside their ken? They are like chaperones charged with protecting a virgin, when everyone in the hotel has a key to her room. They know exactly how often her door opens and closes during the night, but they say nothing.

The high opinion a senior bureaucrat has of himself, and which he cultivates with the greatest of care, prevents him from being aware of his own limitations and therefore guarantees him a relatively large measure of happiness for the foreseeable future. But the fact that this is a fraud perpetrated against himself doesn't quite escape his conscience, so that the smooth ointment of his happiness always contains a small, poisonous fly which, though it doesn't kill him, disturbs his calm, renders him uneasy, testy, jumpy.

∞ ∞ ∞

The senior bureaucrat knows that if he keeps still long enough and doesn't attract too much attention to himself, but doesn't entirely fade from view either, someone presently above him who enjoys solid political or social connections will one day be carried off by sickness, death or promotion. When that happens, someone else might become aware of his presence, make a note of his availability and, out of sheer laziness, or to avoid any bother, or simply because there isn't anyone better handy, toss him the scrap of advancement for which he has waited so long.

∞ ∞ ∞

Senior mandarins have managed to convince the majority of people that there is no such thing as patronage within the Public Service, or at least very little of it, and that the merit principle acts as a kind of antibiotic, searching out and destroying the wicked virus of injustice whenever it rears its ugly head. This is without a doubt the most perfidious deception of the century. And the most successful, for it keeps the TV cameras out of the departmental corridors and in the Houses of Parliament, where they are trained on the poor, naive, inexperienced Cabinet Ministers, who are hounded day and night by the media, and who always seem to have their hands in the till when the lights come on.

∞ ∞ ∞

Among the lower ranks of the Public Service, merit precedes preferment. In the higher echelons, however, merit follows preferment. At least, one hopes it does. If, by some unfortunate chance, merit does not follow preferment, and the chosen candidate subsequently displays no merit whatsoever, the error is corrected by the elimination of the subject, either through lateral transfer or rapid promotion to another section.

∞ ∞ ∞

Those who agree in all matters with a senior bureaucrat are always seen to be the brightest and the best in his eyes. And the purpose of the merit principle is to provide a method by which only the brightest and the best are preferred. What a wonderful coincidence.

∞ ∞ ∞

Elitism, favouritism and friends in high places create senior bureaucrats out of a variety of body shapes and brain sizes, but once they have gained their positions and are no longer in danger of being summarily ousted, a degree of legitimacy is conferred upon them. That is to say, their fellow senior public servants are obliged to recognize and accept them as real, rather than as what they would be seen to be if it were possible to judge them objectively. It is then necessary to wait for a certain period of time before a degree of merit is added to the degree of legitimacy, merit being a quality that is acquired a little at a time — although it is not strictly necessary at all. It is much more important to obtain a position than it is to deserve it.

∞ ∞ ∞

To get promoted, the senior bureaucrat puts more faith in circumstance than in merit. Just as, to get rich, other people put more faith in lotteries than in hard work.

∞ ∞ ∞

The senior bureaucrat has long understood that it is infinitely more important to be well perceived and well received than it is to possess — or even to seem to possess — real worth.

∞ ∞ ∞

After serving out their merit-principle baloney in the staff cafeterias, senior bureaucrats retire to their private dining room to feast on the rare roast beef of caprice, whimsy, power and free will. There, far from the prying eyes and straining ears of the public, the inquiries and interviews of journalists, the analyses and speculations of academics, the one-directional microphones and the infra-red cameras of the security police, they plot the line of their succession, in advance. There, from the closed circle of their friends and protégés, they name the crown princes who will one day sit on their thrones.

∞ ∞ ∞

A hundred years from now, who will know the difference between a senior bureaucrat and the junior clerk buried beside him?

∞ ∞ ∞

Regarded from a great distance, or encountered infrequently, the mandarin assumes a kind of mythical quality. He is bathed in a warm, phosphorescent glow; he acquires a golden aura; he passes into the stuff of legend; he becomes, in short, a god. If, on the other hand, you are brought close to him, or if circumstances force you to remain in his presence day after day after day, his true nature soon supplants the illusory one. Before your very eyes, the god will metamorphose into a satyr, or at the very least into a tragically ordinary mortal. From that moment on, the illusion is irretrievably lost, never to be recaptured. Not even if you once more remove yourself to a great distance, or if you never see him again. The senior bureaucrat is the only mirage on earth that is made of flesh and blood.

One of the few functions fulfilled by the senior bureaucrat is that of helping to keep a certain limited number of elevated thoughts in general circulation. Not his own thoughts, one need hardly add, but thoughts which ought nonetheless to command our attention and admiration. He is rather like the honey bee which, as it flits from flower to flower, unknowingly carries its precious load of pollinating powder stuck to the bottom of its hairy little feet.

∞ ∞ ∞

You may completely ignore the speech of a senior bureaucrat without that nagging sense that you are missing out on something important, that an opportunity for enlightenment is passing you by, or that your mind has been in any way impoverished. No other interlocutor offers you this advantage.

∞ ∞ ∞

Like old maids jealously guarding their secret recipes for hot-rum cakes with frozen chocolate icing, the shining assemblage of senior bureaucrats obstinately clutch to their meagre breasts the formulas of their successes, the reasons for their promotions, the mysteries of their rapid rise through the ranks. They purse their lips, wiggle their elbows, gaze off into space, turn their backs, pretend they are hard of hearing . . . "Tell me, my dear, do you use buckwheat flour? Don't I detect just a hint of burnt sugar?" Come now, gentlemen, don't be shy — tell us about all those grand democratic principles that you defend in the daily accomplishment of your duties, that you try to impart to your subordinates and which, we have no doubt, explain beyond a shadow of a doubt how you have arrived at your present level, and your membership in such a privileged class. Is it because of your competence? No . . . for there are those among you, are there not, who are known far and wide for being complete bungling idiots. Has it to do then with your education? Your experience? Your excellent work record? Years of service? Personality? Strength of character? Intelligence? Ethnic origins? Minority

group? Self-sacrifice? Nationalism? Language? Regional development? The Holy Ghost? . . . Perhaps. Yes, one or the other of
those, or a combination of several, could possibly explain the
presence of some of you at the top of the pyramid, might justify
you calling yourselves senior public servants.

But how do you explain how all those others, year after year,
go on surviving, enduring, existing, hanging on? And, my God,
all those new recruits coming up all the time, so unexpectedly,
so . . . improbably? Where do they fit in? You don't know . . .
Please, you can tell us. Keep your voice down, though — what
about those other reasons we sometimes hear about, late at night,
behind closed doors? You know: things like nepotism, favouritism, friends in high places, intrigues and influence-peddling,
rumours, brown-nosing, manipulations, machinations, subtle
pressurings, politics and politicking, money, sex, partisanship,
ruling classism, hypocrisy, gerrymandering . . . No? Never
heard of them? I thought as much.

∞ ∞ ∞

If he had wings, the senior bureaucrat would be more like a
chicken than an owl, more like an ostrich than an eagle, and
closer to a penguin than a hawk.

∞ ∞ ∞

A senior bureaucrat's reservoir of charm, energy and competence is depleted year by year, until finally it is empty altogether, and he is forced to accept a lesser role, a lower rank, or
even a reduction in pay. His attractions fade, his seductions lose
their guile. He succumbs to the inevitable, like an aging prostitute who wakes up one day, after a long, lonely night, and realizes it is time she became a waitress, or a cleaning lady.

∞ ∞ ∞

In the upper echelons of the Public Service, competence or
its opposite is never the issue.

In the upper echelons of the Public Service, merit is based on the equality of all men. Promotion, however, is based on their inequality.

∞ ∞ ∞

The senior bureaucrat instinctively shuns any system of advancement or promotion that is based on the application of rigid or precisely defined rules. Take seniority, for example: the very word is anathema. You simply add up the fellow's age and years of service, and you have your result. Controversy, uncertainty and unfairness are eliminated with a single stroke of the pen. Wherein lies its gravest danger, since seniority leaves no room for interpretation, hinders all subjective assessment, obstructs the exercise of personal judgement, forces everyone to abide by the same rules, and curtails individual freedom. Seniority is the very death of whimsy; it is poetry's bitterest enemy.

Advancement by merit, however, is the very opposite. Through merit, one escapes the constriction of arithmetic, rationality and regulations. Merit introduces an essential suppleness, it adds a human element, it validates idiosyncrasy, it takes into account the mutability of all living beings, it values hunches, it encourages debate, it allows one to defend one's position and then abandon it altogether: in short, merit is a form of administrative lyricism. Thanks to the principle of advancement by merit, one has the right — nay, the duty — to mull over a thousand and one considerations: I like him, I don't like him, he's my cousin, he's my friend, he smiles too much, he's the least threatening, I owe him a favour, he has a nervous tic, he's a friend of the Deputy Minister, maybe she sleeps around, she gets along well with my brother-in-law, we both like Telemann, we were at McGill together, we were both in London in 1972, she invited me to her last party, she has such a wonderful British accent, he's the Minister's choice, he's not too bright but he has a good personality, her husband drives a BMW, he showed me up at the last finance committee meeting, he knows how to forget that he has a PhD, he's discreet with my secrets and free with everyone else's, he's above average, he works an hour a day longer than his colleagues, he really honks when he blows his nose, she's skied Mont Blanc, he is politically astute, I knew his father well, he comes highly recommended by the former Minister's new wife, he buys only the best Bordeaux, she shops at Bloomingdale's . . .

Merit, then, is the magic word. Merit injects such an essential, human dimension into the development of a senior mandarin's career.

∞ ∞ ∞

The system of patronage as practised by senior bureaucrats has had disastrous unforeseen consequences. Those it pushes too rapidly to the top of the heap suffer from vertigo and a loss of equilibrium, unaccustomed as they are to having recognition and power. Those it precipitates too brusquely to the bottom, on the other hand, become bitter and vengeful, for they can never resign themselves to the anonymous oblivion that awaits them.

∞ ∞ ∞

The mandarin is the only known exception to Newton's first law of physics, for when he falls, he falls up. In fact, not only is he promoted, he is honoured. This defiance of gravity, however, is an affront to nature that must be accepted in silence and serenity, since if one makes the slightest allusion to the recipient's true merit, if one so much as whispers the word "incompetence," one is immediately ostracized as insensitive, lacking in taste, and without a shred of sense in the art of getting ahead. Never, under any circumstance, interfere with the process of deification.

2
Power

꧁꧂

Those who want power, says the senior bureaucrat, should not wait around for it to be handed to them on a platter. Power must be seized — by force, if necessary, by fair means or foul, and no matter what the price. Once you have power, and not a second before, you can start working out compromises with justice, morality, common decency and all those other virtues that, though momentarily outraged by your actions, will sooner or later accommodate themselves to reality — and even collaborate with their new master.

∞ ∞ ∞

Like the enemies of Christopher Columbus, the senior bureaucrat believes he alone stands at the centre of the universe. From the bridge of his little ship, which has slipped its moorings and is being swept along by the outgoing tide, he casts his eye toward land and declares: "See how the earth moves!" And thinks himself an eyewitness to the phenomenon of continental drift.

∞ ∞ ∞

The senior bureaucrat loves situations in which, dashing in at the eleventh hour and, with the magnanimous gesture, the ostentatious and totally arbitrary flourish, he temporarily blocks the normal progression of events. He will nullify the application of a rule, for example, or jam up the normal execution of an operation. He will stop a thing in its tracks, make everyone back up, use his authority to impose a new, totally different direction — a direction, of course, of his own choosing, an expression of his own free will, his own power, his own generosity. He then likes to ride off into the sunset before the beneficiary of his largesse, the unknown citizen who has been spared the blind application of Regulation 9, Section A, Subsection b, Paragraph vii, can shake his hand and say: "Who are you, Masked Man?" No sir, the senior public servant wants no public display of gratitude. Just being able to exercise his power is reward enough. It is a form of transcendental masturbation. It is power performing in a vacuum. It is like revving up the engine of a Ferrari while waiting for the light to change, just for the sheer, subliminal, sensual pleasure of hearing it purr.

∞ ∞ ∞

In the Public Service, to exercise power is almost always to have usurped it. Somewhere, sometime, some way, something illegitimate, dishonest or immoral has taken place, which the mandarin must conceal, particularly from himself.

∞ ∞ ∞

A senior bureaucrat who cannot ensure that an operation will succeed consoles himself with the knowledge that at least he can see that it fails.

∞ ∞ ∞

It is less important to deserve power than it is to show that you can wield it once you have it. That at least is what newly appointed senior public servants would have us believe, in the hope that the fiction will eventually become fact. Or rather in the hope that the fiction will divert attention from the fact.

∞ ∞ ∞

I have learned through the years that power alone leads to the summit of glory, says the senior bureaucrat. All other roads lead only to a plateau.

∞ ∞ ∞

A mandarin likes to think of himself as a free spirit, that the decisions he makes are inspired whims, that they are flowing, spontaneous, unshackled and unfettered emanations of his inner self, pure extensions of his indomitable will, and proof to himself a hundred times over that his power, his impunity, his success soar above the everyday laws of logic and justice — laws that are so mundane, so boring, and yet so completely in control of the conduct of most mortals, who are themselves ordinary, hidebound and pitiable. Not he. He has somehow rediscovered the exuberance of an adolescent, roaring bare-headed and barefooted down the highway in his shiny new convertible, thumbing his nose at the prissy little road signs.

"May I ask, sir, how you came to this decision?"

"Because I felt like it, that's why. Yesterday my judgement might have been swayed by a flash of a woman's thigh, or I may have been moved to pity for a friend in need, or been too conscious of the Minister's wishes, or of the enterprise shown by a junior clerk. But today . . . today I just felt like it. Extraordinary, isn't it? I did it because I wanted to! Step on the gas!"

∞ ∞ ∞

No doubt about it, in the underworld of influence-peddling in which the senior public servant thrives there lurks a conscious and deliberate evil. It is the willful, premeditated, almost joyful miscarriage of justice. The irony is that the ends are often so excellent and justified that few can, in retrospect, find fault with the means. Thus evil passes into good, and makes itself almost lovable.

∞ ∞ ∞

The illusion created by power is so strong that many senior bureaucrats come to believe in their own worth and competence.

There is no more depressing spectacle than that of mediocrity puffed up with power and contentment.

∞ ∞ ∞

The senior bureaucrat knows perfectly well that the difference between truth and falsehood is negligible, if it exists at all, and rests solely on one's own perception of things, ideas or events. It would no doubt be foolhardy to deny clear evidence, to insist that a thing is black when it is obviously white. But in life there very seldom *is* any clear evidence, and the only discernible colour is grey. Having perceived this truism, the senior public servant sets about bringing opposites together, placing a dimmer-switch, as it were, on the harsh light of reality. The difficulty is that he is always performing before a trick mirror, in which he sees what appears to be the truth but which is almost imperceptibly altered by a succession of concave and convex curves and corrugations. A cat still looks like a cat, and a chair looks like a chair. No denying it. But what a monstrous cat, and what an unlikely chair. The deformities, at once repulsive and laughable, can be attractive . . . even seductive.

The senior bureaucrat thus becomes a plastic surgeon of the abstract, moulding, touching up, shaping and changing that which is revealed to him in the mirror. He makes the obese appear thin, the dwarf seem gigantic; he gives shoulder blades to the hunchback, perky little breasts to the hag, a flowing mane to the baldpated; he plumps out curves and redistributes flesh. The reverse, of course, is also within his powers. The haughty secretary can be made to look ugly; the sparkle in the eye of an over-zealous assistant is given a sinister lustre; a pleasant, open face is turned into a sarcastic mask; the athletic physique of a rival is made perfectly unremarkable; a friendly smile becomes a psychotic grimace; and the ordinary ears on the head of an unfavoured candidate swell to hideous proportions.

∞ ∞ ∞

True laziness in the Public Service is found only among the lower ranks. Senior mandarins have stages of research, reflection and consultation, exploratory gatherings, information meetings, debriefing sessions, gestation periods, preliminary observations and delegations of authority. The end result is the same — inaction followed by a complete lack of productivity — but the process is viewed from a more positive angle, and is thereby ennobled.

∞ ∞ ∞

When you have lived cheek-by-jowl with senior mandarins for a long time, and then have moved away some distance, it is like waking up from a long sleep. Suddenly, you understand the absolute necessity — the terrible urgency — of establishing some kind of buffer zone, in the form of unions or syndicates, to protect the hapless individual, however imperfectly, from the capers of the senior public servants' egotistical will.

∞ ∞ ∞

Rank confers on senior bureaucrats the divine right to deliver long and loud speeches, to be correct every single time they open their mouths, and to translate their most whimsical desires into immediate action. It is of secondary importance to know whether or not they are speaking intelligently, or if the decisions they make are the best possible under the circumstances. In fact, it has been proven beyond all reasonable doubt that the most horrendous mistakes affect the status of the senior bureaucrat not a whit. This is because there is no connection at all between power and those who wield it, even though it is generally — though wrongly — supposed that the latter leads to the former, and that the former is a natural and logical consequence of the latter. You may put your heads together and ask yourselves why this is so . . . No one, it seems, will have an answer. One plausible explanation is that humanity, for those who believe in the hierarchization of human beings according to their abilities, is still in its embryonic, infantile stage, no more advanced than it was a few centuries ago when madmen were thrown into jail, the earth was believed to be flat, and witches were burned at the stake. Or when, even earlier, men used their muscles to impose their points of view, their decisions, or their will, on other, weaker, but more intelligent, men. Evolution may be taking place, but its rhythm is funereal. We are still lost somewhere between brawn and brain.

∞ ∞ ∞

The aging mandarin seeks out every possible occasion on which to exercise his will, in order to prove to anyone who happens to be watching that the old internal drive is still strong within him. His actual actions may be directed at any random object, may lean toward efficacy or veer toward incompetence, may court good or evil, appear black or white. It is the act of aiming that is important; any target at all will do.

∞ ∞ ∞

Knowing that a good man is often perceived as being an innocent, and therefore undeserving of power, and not wanting to appear to be incapable of malice, the senior bureaucrat from time to time applies himself diligently to being malicious. It goes against his natural inclination, to be sure, but it demonstrates that he is not a slave to goodness, and that he is therefore deserving of power.

∞ ∞ ∞

The senior bureaucrat would rather be powerful than competent. When power is not available, however, he would rather be competent than powerless. Who could have any objections?

∞ ∞ ∞

When all is said and done, the only real fault to be found in a senior bureaucrat is that he is like a spoiled child. But when one has known the giddiness that goes with the exercise of power, the free play of authority, the complete lack of moral restraint, the triumph of whimsy, the promiscuity of greatness, the impunity of position, the easy relations between men of good will, the intimate conversations with decision-makers, how difficult it is to bring oneself back down to life on a minor scale, to be compelled by boring equality, colourless merit and dull justice.

∞ ∞ ∞

A senior bureaucrat will go to great lengths to appear more powerful than he actually is. There is the same satisfaction, but without the need to devote the effort, time and energy required to become powerful in fact. Nor is there the long, nerve-wracking wait for that one stroke of luck that will make him powerful beyond his wildest dreams. If you can fool them with paste, why buy diamonds?

You think you've got him this time. You can already see him squirming on the pin. You hold in your hand a piece of uncontrovertible reality, a pure, naked chunk of evidence that no one in his right mind can deny. It is round, black, hard and very heavy. You show it to the senior bureaucrat, triumphant, calm in the knowledge that there is no longer anything to explain, to defend, to prove. You are wrong. He looks at it without emotion, without surprise, almost without interest. He simply denies it. He, too, is calm. He is serene. Impassive. He denies its shape, its colour, its density, its weight. He is beyond reality. He ignores it. He reconstructs it, adapts it to his own perception, to his own will, to an Ideal Form that exists only in his own mind. The real world is obliterated and remade every second. He points out to you the square, white, soft and weightless object that you are holding in the palm of your hand.

∞ ∞ ∞

The senior bureaucrat endures the tyranny of his superiors only in the hope of one day becoming a tyrant himself.

∞ ∞ ∞

Once he realizes he *can* do something, the senior bureaucrat stops wondering if he *should* do it; he does it. For power assured of impunity has no use for legitimacy.

In the Public Service, hierarchy prevails over justice. When, after having tried in vain to redress a wrong that has been done to him, the junior clerk takes his complaint directly to a senior bureaucrat, the latter's only response is to deliver a severe dressing-down for arrogance and insubordination. The clerk has not attained sufficient social or organizational status to appeal to a higher authority.

"You must learn to accept the measure of justice that is your due," says the mandarin.

∞   ∞   ∞

To a senior bureaucrat in a position of authority, reason and justice are malleable concepts susceptible to infinitesimal modifications, gradually changing in colour and shape until they conform to his own will. This metamorphosis is so successful, so imperceptible, that it takes a highly discerning mind to distinguish the fakes from the originals. The senior public servant's mind, it need hardly be said, is incapable of such discernment.

∞   ∞   ∞

As well as being chief administrative officer of his department, the senior bureaucrat is also its chief judge. This happy combination of roles makes his job so much easier, since it means that as judge he alone evaluates the decisions he makes as an administrator. This symbiotic relationship between the two functions has some interesting side effects: it saves time, it facilitates communication between different levels of bureaucracy, it increases understanding and harmony within the department, and it keeps disagreements and friction to a bare minimum.

∞   ∞   ∞

Most senior bureaucrats have only enough power to do themselves justice.

∞   ∞   ∞

Qualifications for a Deputy Minister, apart from a minimal amount of competence and leadership ability: (1) He must have an innate and instinctive taste for remorseless cruelty, which he must be able to indulge spontaneously, at a moment's notice, in such a way as to provoke a high degree of anxiety in his employees, thus terrorizing them into a constant state of alertness. (2) He must know how to catch people off-guard. (3) He must be adept at avoiding situations involving reason or logic, in which he may be caught off-guard himself. (4) He must be entirely self-assured when handing down decisions that bear absolutely no weight and lead to no outcome. (5) He must recognize that generosity of spirit and a friendly manner are weaknesses inconsistent with the exercise of power.

∞ ∞ ∞

The senior bureaucrat takes up a double-edged sword and runs his thumb along one edge: it cuts. He runs his thumb along the other edge: it cuts just as deeply. He smiles. The double-edged sword is his mind. He can hack away with either side. The yes side, the no side. Yes, no, no, yes. Heads or tails. Eenie, meenie, minie, moe.

∞ ∞ ∞

The senior mandarin believes that he has a kind of divine right to arbitrate, and that injustice is an integral part of arbitration. This right is inalienable, natural, immutable, and subject to neither reproach nor revoke. It is an autonomous verity, an objective and independent fact that is inscribed into the normal order of things and against which even he has no appeal. It is a force greater than himself (the only one he acknowledges). It is his by right of birth. It never occurs to him that exercising this divine right could have any but desirable results. When it has, he convinces himself that undesirable results are an unfortunate but negligible consequence of power, necessary accidents. He believes, obscurely, that since he must view things from such an elevated height, he cannot be held responsible for the details, for the dust that is kicked up from the road over which he is driven. If you persist, if you charge him formally with committing an error, of not being impartial, of making an arbitrary decision, he will be the most astounded of men; his eyes will widen with offended innocence, he will bluster that you have called into question his ability to run his department, his fiefdom, that you have knocked the very breath from his holy person, that he cannot continue to live for another second unless you withdraw this attack against his integrity, his very being, his divine right to be right, his power to transform his every gesture, no matter how lowly, into the purest virtue . . .

∞ ∞ ∞

The senior bureaucrat has no fear of common sense.

∞ ∞ ∞

When he is attacked, the senior bureaucrat will turn to the government arsenal to defend himself. The weapons therein are effective, cost him nothing, and he has no trouble justifying his use of them.

∞ ∞ ∞

The senior bureaucrat is profoundly convinced that authority is a proper substitute for justice, and power for common sense.

∞ ∞ ∞

Between common sense and the opinions of a senior mandarin there is no contest.

∞ ∞ ∞

The senior bureaucrat will laugh along with you, indeed will laugh harder than you, at the scourge of red tape that paralyzes his administrative universe. But deep down he is not laughing at all. He only pretends to laugh at red tape, in order to please you. To make you think that he agrees with you. In reality, the administrative constipation is a source of deep satisfaction to him: red is the only true colour in his otherwise irremediably grey realm.

The pleasure of seeing someone waiting in a chair outside his office. Of watching the snow slowly melt from his boots to form round, dark stains on the government carpet. While nothing else moves. Of listening to the endless electronic rhythm of a Xerox machine in the next room. The sound of paper sliding over paper, of paper folding, of paper tearing. While nothing at all is happening anywhere. Of hearing a telephone ringing and ringing at the end of the hall, and no one picking it up. Of hearing his secretary repeat yet again the standardized lie: "No, I'm sorry, he's in a meeting . . ." Of experiencing the exquisite rapture of inactivity, which produces its most intense euphoria only when one knows for certain that someone, at that precise moment, is waiting for one to act. Of being watched in turn by the tired, bored and uncomprehending eyes of someone who is waiting for his summons. Patiently. Obsequiously. The little world of the polite and the correct. While his own eyes, the serene, sloe, impassive eyes of the senior bureaucrat, watch the smoke outside his window rising from a factory on the flats below. Or from the exhausts of all those cars stopped at the red light, all of them, like the fellow outside his door, waiting so patiently for the light to change. They wait, as he enjoys the spectacle.

∞ ∞ ∞

The mandarin loves to avail himself of the unspoken honour, the tacit privilege, that allows him to contravene with impunity the rules that govern lesser mortals. Or at least twist and bend them to his own use. For him, all subordinates lower their eyes and voices out of respect, even with pleasure. The senior bureaucrat expects nothing less from them.

∞ ∞ ∞

There is a technique used in painting called *en abîme* in which one sees a mirror, and in the mirror a woman holding a mirror, and in that mirror the same woman holding the same mirror, and so on and so on. In just such a way is the senior bureaucrat a perfect reflection of himself repeated *ad infinitum* to form a kind of super-anonymity, a sort of safety in numbers, in which each image blends with the others, thus rendering them all impregnable to attack. No clear target presents itself to your sights. It is perpetually out of focus. And you do not know who to blame, who is at fault, who is responsible. Not this one — this one, no — that one, no . . .

3
Competence

∞∞∞

Competence in a senior bureaucrat is not so much a measure of what he can do as of what he can avoid doing.

∞ ∞ ∞

Senior public servants excel at lining up ideas end to end, but they have great difficulty integrating one set of ideas into another. They are also adept at reducing an idea to its component parts, but cannot then put it back together again into its original form. Finally, they have no trouble grouping ideas randomly, but only rarely are they capable of organizing them according to shape, size, weight or order of importance.

Chimpanzees have the same problem with boxes, cubes, cylinders and circles of coloured cardboard, which they are given to manipulate in order to measure their intelligence and manual dexterity.

∞ ∞ ∞

In the good old days, complains the senior bureaucrat, I was often wrong by being right too soon. These days, I'm often wrong by being right too late.

∞ ∞ ∞

a. By feigning competence, the senior bureaucrat eventually becomes competent.

b. By feigning competence, the senior bureaucrat eventually has to feign competence all the time.

There is nothing wrong with the first scenario, but the second is more common.

∞ ∞ ∞

The senior bureaucrat cannot sustain a philosophical discussion for very long without succumbing to mental fatigue, to a kind of intellectual vertigo, which renders him completely and utterly useless. His motor-drive quickly becomes overheated. If, upon perceiving this, and out of compassion for his agitation of mind, you offer him a concrete example to illustrate your position, you will have committed a serious error. For the moment you offer him this charitable perch, he will pounce upon it violently and cling to it for dear life. He will see nothing but your example, he will talk of nothing else, he will force you to abandon the real subject of your conversation in order to dwell exclusively on your own example, with which he feels perfectly at home and which has allowed him to regain his breath after such a long, lofty flight into the intellectual stratosphere.

Furthermore, if you are so unwise as to finish a sentence with a phrase such as ". . . you'd be wasting your time, it'd be like going for a cruise on the Titanic," then you are well and truly lost. Immediately, a host of maritime images will flood into his brain, dark waves will rise and submerge everything in their wake, thick fog will drift in and cloud his vision. Sooner or later, the inevitable question will float to the top:

"So, you like sailing too?"

You can try to backtrack, to explain that you were just using an example, a figure of speech, probably not a very good one at that. But it won't do you any good. You can interrupt him, talk over him, shout at him — nothing will work. Your conversation will never return to where you left it. The senior bureaucrat will never again allow you to climb back up to the dry, Saharan dunes of the intellect. You can't beat him, so you might as well join him:

"What do you have, a single-keel or a catamaran?"

∞ ∞ ∞

After a thousand attempts and nine hundred and ninety-nine failures, the senior bureaucrat will finally succeed in doing what was not worth the effort in the first place.

∞ ∞ ∞

At first, the senior bureaucrat hasn't the faintest hint of an idea. But he doodles something on a scrap of paper, or tosses a few words into a dictaphone, and they bounce around, rebound off one another, rub shoulders, come together, then finally give birth to a full-blown, fortuitous, accidental, novel and completely unexpected idea. This the senior bureaucrat clasps to his breast and cherishes as his own, as a mother cherishes her child without comprehending in the slightest the complex genetic miracle that has taken place within her.

∞ ∞ ∞

The senior public servant who has fallen into disfavour rarely rises again to his former eminence. Like matches, virginity and Kleenex, he is used once, then tossed away.

∞ ∞ ∞

After a lengthy and laborious deliberation of the problem you have put to him, the senior bureaucrat is finally on the verge of delivering a response. But then, at the last moment, he asks you for a point of clarification which clearly indicates that he hasn't understood the matter at all, so that you have to begin all over again. It is like waiting all morning for toast to pop up in a toaster that isn't plugged in.

∞ ∞ ∞

You've heard about "high fliers" in the Public Service? Don't believe everything you hear. The only things that fly high in the public servant's sky are vultures. Eagles wouldn't bother with such a desolate place. Besides, they prefer fresh meat to carrion.

The senior mandarin prefers talking and acting to thinking. He associates talking and acting with pleasure; thinking, to him, is a form of pain.

∞ ∞ ∞

To err is human, certainly. But to err on a monumental scale requires either a computer or a senior bureaucrat.

∞ ∞ ∞

If senior bureaucrats are in a hurry, it is because there are always delays. And if there are delays, it is because senior bureaucrats are always in a hurry.

∞ ∞ ∞

It is not by doing nothing that the senior bureaucrat causes foul-ups. It is by putting himself into motion. The harmonious universe tumbles into chaos, a single discord makes itself heard, and a series of useless gestures ripples outward. Motion, in a senior bureaucrat, is like the birth of a wave in the Sargasso Sea: it disturbs everything around it for months before it finally subsides on the shore.

∞ ∞ ∞

When he looks back, the senior bureaucrat can easily prove that he was right. Similarly, when he looks ahead, he can always demonstrate that he will be right. The problem — and it is an irritating one — is that he is never right at the moment.

∞ ∞ ∞

The senior bureaucrat knows instinctively that he must never become indispensable or irreplaceable. If he were, he would never be promoted.

∞ ∞ ∞

Agreement among senior public servants is often the result of a misunderstanding. So is disagreement.

∞ ∞ ∞

When a senior bureaucrat cannot do a thing himself, he has it done for him. But not for an instant does he doubt his own ability to judge the results obtained by those who knew how to do the thing, and did it.

∞ ∞ ∞

When a senior public servant looks for something in his right-hand drawer, it is usually in his left-hand drawer. And vice versa.

∞ ∞ ∞

There is only one explanation when a senior bureaucrat gets something right the first time: he did something wrong.

∞ ∞ ∞

If electricity could be generated from inertia, senior bureaucrats would be rich.

∞ ∞ ∞

If in the mind of a senior bureaucrat you are an incompetent, be happy. It is the opposite that should concern you.

∞ ∞ ∞

Whatever a senior public servant undertakes requires just a little more time to complete than he thought it would.

∞ ∞ ∞

The senior bureaucrat never has enough time to do a thing properly. But he always has enough time to start the thing again.

The senior bureaucrat cheerfully admits that he does nothing at all, but insists that he does it better than anyone else.

∞ ∞ ∞

Incompetence, says the senior public servant, is not something one is born with. It is something one achieves!

∞ ∞ ∞

One of the advantages enjoyed by senior mandarins is to be naturally safe from plagiarism and theft of intellectual property.

∞ ∞ ∞

Life can sometimes teach some hard lessons. The senior bureaucrat, for example, learns the hard way that he has only himself to rely on, and that the sooner he learns to live with that handicap, the better.

∞ ∞ ∞

The senior bureaucrat rushes to defend anything that is acceptable, anything that, while not being actively bad, at least falls far short of excellent.

∞ ∞ ∞

The senior bureaucrat speaks little and writes less, except for what is useless, which spews out of him profusely. He also thinks little but long; long enough, at any rate, to allow the due course of time to render a difficult decision superfluous. To a senior bureaucrat, deep reflection takes the form of a slow, meditative masturbation leading to a perpetually postponed orgasm.

∞ ∞ ∞

No use denying the evidence: senior public servants whose vision is beyond question are ahead of their time by several hours.

Waiters wait, boxers box and thinkers think. Do not conclude from this, however, that senior public servants serve.

∞ ∞ ∞

Senior bureaucrats move about in the Public Service like flies in a car speeding down the highway. They buzz aimlessly and quietly about, caught up in their own world, unaware that that world is whisking them along at an unbelievable pace, a pace they could not hope to attain on their own.

∞ ∞ ∞

The mandarin accepts without the slightest demur the accolades of those who assume that his success is the result of his own actions, his own experience, or his own talent. He knows perfectly well that the one who truly deserves the congratulations — Blind Chance — will never speak up and demand his share of the glory. It is like stealing from no one . . . Who's to know?

∞ ∞ ∞

You must not allow your surprise to show if a senior bureaucrat takes you aside and quietly, modestly but quite shamelessly assures you that he is far superior to certain, or even all, of his colleagues, either in general or in a particular instance. Certainly it is odd behaviour, and quite childish. But be patient with him. After all, if he doesn't take on the task — and it is a task — of patting himself on the back from time to time, who would do it for him? Would you?

∞ ∞ ∞

The mind of a senior bureaucrat works in much the same way as his eyes. His eyes require a certain period of time to adjust to a sudden change in light, whether darker or brighter than it was before. Similarly, his mind needs time to adapt to a new idea, especially if it is a more difficult concept to grasp than the simple, familiar pablum upon which he has fed for so many years.

The senior bureaucrat can instantly call up a whole arsenal of arguments to prove that such-and-such a solution was either the worst possible or the best imaginable. He excels in contrariety, he is the master of opposites. He is a flashlight that projects a beam of darkness.

∞ ∞ ∞

When he reaches a level of mere competence, the senior bureaucrat thinks he has achieved genius.

∞ ∞ ∞

Rather than have you repeat something for the fourth time, the senior public servant will pretend that he finally understands what you have said. He smiles and nods, but watch him closely: his eyes are troubled and questioning.

∞ ∞ ∞

The senior bureaucrat is never competent unless there are witnesses.

∞ ∞ ∞

According to the Peter Principle, one is promoted until one reaches one's level of incompetence. After that, it is presumed that one is no longer promoted. Wrong. The senior bureaucrat is living proof that one can be promoted far, far beyond this level, and for years after it has been reached. The reason for this is simply that those who have the power to promote him are ahead of him on the ladder, and, by virtue of the same Peter Principle, have therefore themselves been promoted to a much higher level of incompetence. Promotion in the Public Service is a bit like the calculation of compound interest, or a geometric progression, in the sense that there are not only higher but *greater* levels of incompetence as one approaches the summit of the pyramid. From this we may infer a new Peter Principle: The higher an incompetent is promoted, the more likely he is to be promoted again.

Balance and equilibrium, which the senior mandarin looks for in all things, are incompatible with feelings and passion. As a result, his motivation becomes totally cerebral, abstract, theoretical, and bereft of emotion in all things, large or small. This reduces the chances of error, certainly, but it also eliminates the possibility of glory and excellence.

∞ ∞ ∞

When the senior bureaucrat tries to harmonize what he is with what he appears to be, he finds that he lacks the ear for it. He cannot detect and correct the dissonance, the subtle cacophony, the annoying distortion. The imitation is good, and has fooled more than a few, but anyone with a fine ear will become impatient and annoyed. The two tracks will sound out of sync.

∞ ∞ ∞

Senior public servants die like fish. When confronted by an obstacle that prevents them from going in a certain direction, they persist in trying to go in that direction anyway. Like cod drowning in a gill-net.

∞ ∞ ∞

The senior bureaucrat never fully succeeds in becoming what he would have us believe he is, but the effort and its frustration are his constant companions. The result is an air of falsity that permeates his entire being and impregnates his every move. The sheep's clothing can never quite hide the wolf beneath. In the end, one gives up expecting perfection, a totally successful seeming, and accepts the senior bureaucrat for what he truly is: a person who is constantly trying to be someone or something that he is not, but who, like a failed magician, can never create a convincing illusion, can never find the rabbit in the top hat.

∞ ∞ ∞

When he speaks, the senior bureaucrat fills with words the gaping holes in his memory and in his knowledge. In both cases, the important thing is not to let the gaps show.

∞ ∞ ∞

The senior public servant specializes, in fact excels, in knowing instinctively what to do in order to be promoted. Once he has been promoted, however, he is lost, spent. Getting promoted is his one and only talent.

∞ ∞ ∞

If, when listening to a senior bureaucrat, you give him your entire attention and expend upon him every last ounce of your good will, he will afterwards say that you are very well spoken.

∞ ∞ ∞

In the mandarinate, charisma is often a successful substitute for competence. So successful, in fact, that it is common to find a powerful personality filling a position about which he knows absolutely nothing, and which inspires in him nothing but a deep and thinly disguised contempt. Still, charismatic incompetence is not so dreaded a disease that every senior bureaucrat doesn't dream of catching it some day.

∞ ∞ ∞

When a senior public servant talks about incompetence, it goes without saying that he is talking about someone else's incompetence.

∞ ∞ ∞

The senior bureaucrat produces nothing. Or very little. Most often, all his activities, intense though they certainly are, lead nowhere, have no outlet in anything that can be seen, felt or appreciated. Hence his respect for routines, regulations, forms and authorizations. And with what aplomb, what panache, what elegance, does he go frantically about producing nothing.

∞ ∞ ∞

Do you want to know why a senior bureaucrat never goes into a project full steam ahead? Because by so doing he would be demonstrating the limits of his abilities. This would be a grievous error. Nothing is more dangerous to one who hopes to climb up the ladder than to let it be seen or heard that there are limits to one's abilities, and that one has arrived at these limits.

∞ ∞ ∞

When earning your living condemns you to daily contact with the same senior bureaucrats, you should read a few pages of Nietzsche every evening. Or see a black-and-white Bergman film. Or listen to Saint-Saëns' symphony for organ. These are all difficult works, and they will form a counter-weight, a kind of antidote, to the conversations you will have at the office, and to the vacuous, frivolous and soul-destroying tasks you will have to perform there. Otherwise you will suffer from a strong sense of deprivation, as if your idle brain is becoming corroded, thickened and diminished.

∞ ∞ ∞

The senior public servant does well what he ought not to do at all. Sometimes he does it badly, too.

∞ ∞ ∞

Senior bureaucrats affect competence the way some women wear lipstick. It becomes them even when, strictly speaking, it is unnecessary. But to the majority of senior bureaucrats, incompetence is a definite advantage, just as for a woman the absence of lipstick can accentuate the natural colour and beauty of her lips. In general, senior bureaucrats leave competence to those who actually need it — junior clerks, for example, who have no other way of getting ahead. They are like rich aristocrats who leave the hammer-and-tong work to the lower classes.

∞ ∞ ∞

Public servants who wish to become senior public servants are strongly advised to choose for themselves a mentor, a godfather, a protector, one of the mandarins of the service who has considerable weight and authority and is willing to wield it at opportune moments on his protégé's behalf. In matters of advancement, the ends always justify the means so long as the means exhibit a certain amount of taste and discretion. If virtue and ability are insufficient to guarantee the desired results, it is well to have surer, more effective means to fall back on.

∞ ∞ ∞

Anything that is simple and clear in the mind of a senior bureaucrat is usually inapplicable in reality.

∞ ∞ ∞

Extraordinary qualities of mind and profundity of soul are not what one looks for in a candidate for promotion within the Public Service. Excellence itself is a form of excess, and excess dangerously undermines the values prized by the Public Service. A state-of-the-art car engine, for example, can perform too well, thereby posing a serious threat not only to the body in which it is installed, but also to the other, slower, vehicles that plod along the streets and highways. The excellence of such an engine is demonstrated by its smooth running, aggressive passing, hurtling speeds and an unheard-of life expectancy. Unfortunately, these qualities are incompatible with the regularity of the bureaucratic mechanism, whose greatest virtues are regularity, stolidity, constancy and repetition. In short, the perfect senior bureaucrat is, paradoxically, not the one who aspires to perfection, but the one who most nearly approaches the norm, and stays there.

∞ ∞ ∞

New senior bureaucrats ignore the wisdom and experience of others and insist on making their own mistakes as a necessary part of their apprenticeship. Strictly speaking, this is commendable. The trouble is, however, that they all seem to make them at the same time.

∞ ∞ ∞

An opinion held by a senior bureaucrat is often no more than the verbal expression of a regulation. In a senior bureaucrat, memory, not intelligence, precedes thought.

∞ ∞ ∞

The senior mandarin in his office is like a eunuch in a harem: he no longer knows what it is he is supposed to be doing, nor how to go about doing it. In any case, he lacks the necessary equipment. In spite of this, however, he pretends to teach others how to do it, and to judge their results.

∞ ∞ ∞

Teilhard de Chardin has suggested that birds' wings, bees' hives and the tiger's fangs represent a perfection that is at once relative and definitive, in that although these attributes ensure the animals' survival, they prohibit them from evolving to an even greater perfection — for example, the blossoming of intelligence. In just such a way the public servant who expresses himself well, does his job with an excess of competence and quickly raises himself in the estimation of his superiors, ensures that he will never rise to a higher rung on the ladder. This is because his superiors, convinced that this model employee will continue to do well, will focus all of their attention on other, less gifted employees, those whose potential is preserved intact, whose available energy remains untapped, whose ignorance and incompetence leave plenty of room for growth, and who have successfully avoided the dead end of small perfections, thereby making themselves immediate candidates for higher hierarchical flowerings.

∞ ∞ ∞

The best senior bureaucrats know very well that they are failures. The worst do not know this, and continue to behave as if
nothing ever goes wrong.

∞ ∞ ∞

No member of the human race works as long and as successfully as the senior bureaucrat does to prove his critics right.

∞ ∞ ∞

Whether it is simply an anatomical anomaly, a particular
mental deficiency, or a form of atrophy brought on by his official
duties, the senior bureaucrat, unlike most human beings, lacks
the ability to step outside himself, to observe his own functioning with an objective eye. He is incapable of making such a difficult transformation, of seeing himself as others see him, of as-
suming the dual role of observer and observed. He cannot step
through the looking glass, or follow the perimeter of a vicious
circle. The advantage of this physiological defect is that it confers
upon the senior bureaucrat an endearing lack of complexity, an
attractive simplicity, since our minds can more easily apprehend
and manipulate space that has been robbed of its third dimension. Few of us, however, envy this state of happiness. We seek
a more demanding, a more challenging paradise.

∞ ∞ ∞

In some games, the winner is the one who accumulates the
most points. In other games, the goal is to gain as few points as
possible. The senior bureaucrat excels in the latter.

∞ ∞ ∞

The senior bureaucrat writes and speaks for no other reason
than to be understood. What would be the point, he says, of
using a highly perfected, more powerful transmitter when all his
colleagues are equipped with outmoded receivers of feeble capacity and a limited range of frequencies? His colleagues, for
their part, have no intention of wasting money on more modern,

ultra-sensitive receivers when they know that such equipment would far surpass the degree of efficiency and refinement required to receive the kind of rudimentary messages of which the senior bureaucrat's transmitter is capable. Thus is the delicate balance of mediocrity perpetuated.

∞ ∞ ∞

In the Public Service, mental acuity acts like a thermometer in the Arctic. Even on the warmest, sunniest days it hovers around the freezing point. In vain does one hope for a current of warm air that will send the thin red line of mercury shooting skywards. In the end, one resigns oneself to the permafrost and finds comfort in the muddy soil that marks an incertain and all too brief summer. One dreams of a land somewhere to the south where the spirit can soar.

4
The Economy

Economists always marvel at facts. It is such a relief for them to be able to leave behind their dull, grey uncertainties, if only for a few brief moments.

∞ ∞ ∞

One of the chief advantages of the recent progress in economics is all the new jobs it has created for economists.

∞ ∞ ∞

Senior economists have pulled off a marvellous magical trick: they have given their mistakes a noble air of legitimacy. People even get angry at events for not taking place as the economists predicted.

∞ ∞ ∞

Why does the economist sound so confident and sure when he makes his pronouncements? Because he knows none of them can be checked.

∞ ∞ ∞

Search high and low, you will not find the economist you had lunch with a year ago whose predictions for the future were made with such élan.

The worst epidemic among economists is amnesia. They never remember a thing they said last year about the economy this year, and if they do recall a small part of it, this never coincides with the part you remember. If, however, by some unfortunate stroke of luck, your own memory of their pronouncements is a bit hazy, or if they can establish that you were not present when they made them, then their memories will improve at a stupefying rate.

∞ ∞ ∞

Economists should be treated like prophets: never pay them in advance.

∞ ∞ ∞

Economists know perfectly well that they do not deserve the attention and respect we give them. But they also know how much depends on keeping the myth alive.

5
Management

❧

Modern theories of management are like desert flowers — they pop up, flower, and fade away within a very short space of time. The actual efficacy of management, meanwhile, is improved not a whit. These theories do serve, however, to create more buzz words and exciting neologisms that nurture nothing but snobbery. Senior bureaucrats, therefore, study them avidly. The latest theory is snatched up and bandied about before the ink is even dry on the memo sheet. In this way, the senior bureaucrat shows himself to be one of the avant-garde, to have a mind open to new ideas, to willingly accept change, and even to possess a certain youthfulness and vitality of spirit. After a year or two, however, when the new theory has begun to wane, to lack piquancy, he is the first to drop it in favour of a newer adventure. In the meantime, the ordinary, everyday, garden-variety management goes about its business in its usual way.

∞ ∞ ∞

As long as you carry out my orders, says the senior bureaucrat, I don't need to know how you do it. In fact, I don't *want* to know how you do it. That way, if something goes wrong I can say it wasn't my fault in a much more convincing manner. When innocence is impossible, the next best thing is ignorance.

∞ ∞ ∞

To the senior bureaucrat, it is not important that a fixed objective is not reached, as long as the failure to reach it is accomplished according to the rules. If, by following the rules, the objective is reached, so much the better. But that is a completely accidental by-product of following the rules. It is totally unacceptable to reach an objective by breaking the rules. To a senior bureaucrat, means are always more important than ends.

∞ ∞ ∞

A sense of moderation and balance is so predominant in a senior bureaucrat that he almost never uses exclamation points. Ellipses, on the other hand . . . these show up all the time . . . to mark a gap in the smooth functioning of his . . . brain . . . to betray a momentary blip in his mental processes . . . to serve notice that he is about to begin talking again . . . that he is going to try once more to unravel the unfinished yet endless ball of yarn that is his hesitant . . . searching . . . thought.

∞ ∞ ∞

The senior bureaucrat's universe is not demanding. One can get along quite nicely just by keeping on one's toes, waiting for an opportunity, holding oneself in readiness for one of those lucky shots that fate regularly throws into one's path when one hangs around in the right places. Just as a flycatcher, settled comfortably on its sunny perch, waits for the wind and chance to bring its dinner: when an insect happens along, the flycatcher reaches up and snaps. No big deal. Only a small flutter of its wings.

∞ ∞ ∞

People will drown you with new ideas, says the senior bureaucrat, if you let them.

∞ ∞ ∞

In the buildings occupied by the great Clerks of State, the light always comes from below, so that the occupants' heads are always the last to be illuminated. Like heat, bureaucratic darkness accumulates near the ceiling.

∞ ∞ ∞

Objections put forward by a senior bureaucrat have the same effect on an idea as mud has on a foot. So that, when he argues persuasively, the idea is sucked to the bottom of the bog and is lost forever.

∞ ∞ ∞

No matter what happens, the senior bureaucrat can do nothing about it. That's the way it is, and you might as well accept it. He is powerless in the face of the vast administrative machine that he and his colleagues, past and present, have constructed over the years and which they tend day after day without having the slightest control over its direction or velocity. He merely clings to it, and allows himself to be dragged along at a hellish pace toward an unknown destination. If you have a complaint, it is useless to bring it to him. He will understand your problem perfectly; he will sympathize with your point of view, encourage you in your revolt, and share in your anguish at the trials and tribulations to which you have been subjected. But then he will tell you he is as incapable as you are of altering the course of the runaway dinosaur he has created. He will, however, advise you to resign yourself to your fate, to look for the silver lining, and even, taking heart against a sea of troubles, try to cheer you up with amusing little anecdotes about the interminable carousel-ride to which you are both condemned.

∞ ∞ ∞

If things were left to chance, everyone would be better off. Now, if we could just find something else for the senior bureaucrats to do . . .

∞ ∞ ∞

The senior bureaucrat is proud of his inability to write, and happily delegates that boring, thankless task to his junior clerk as a function too menial for a superior brain such as his. Once relieved of that burden, he is free to carry out without hindrance the higher pursuits to which his exalted rank entitles him: the generation and articulation of great thoughts, for example, the formulation of concepts so innovative, so noble, so profound, so abstract, so difficult, so hard-hitting . . . Ah! If only one could think without using words! Words are so hard to understand and control.

∞ ∞ ∞

The senior official knows from experience that if he allows the pile of papers accumulating in his in-tray to get high enough, then events or simply the inexorable passage of time will render them out-dated, inoffensive and useless. All he has to do then is have them filed away and close the file.

∞ ∞ ∞

At first it makes the mandarin uneasy, then he becomes anxious, and finally he is terrified: every day, when turning a corner in the corridor, or at some other time when he least expects it, but more and more frequently, it seems to him, though he is still taken completely by surprise, he meets the dark, unmoving, grinning ghost of Kafka, who stares at him but never says a word.

∞ ∞ ∞

Only when it is obviously too late does the senior bureaucrat get down to some serious work.

∞ ∞ ∞

Management to a senior bureaucrat is like ballroom dancing: before he makes a move he has to know where to put his feet. The risk of stepping on someone's toes is greatly diminished, but so too is any possibility of style and grace.

The recently promoted senior bureaucrat regards the rules laid down by his predecessors as a kind of challenge, like hurdles strewn in his path by mischievous but playful little elves. He allows himself to be drawn into the game like a kitten attracted by a ball of yarn. Calling on his inner resources, he weaves around the first obstacle, hops over the second, neatly sidesteps the third, ignores the fourth, and continues around the track like a racehorse in a steeplechase. The more he refuses to comply with the rules of the game, the more admiration he draws from his colleagues who, less enterprising, less audacious, less imaginative than he is, have allowed themselves without protest to be governed by them.

∞ ∞ ∞

Delegating authority, in the mind of the senior bureaucrat, is not just a wise administrative principle; often it is simply an excuse to display his power over others; and sometimes it is a downright attempt to get out of doing something himself. Which is why he will always choose to have a thing done for him rather than do it himself. Except in sexual encounters, of course.

∞ ∞ ∞

The main accomplishment of a senior bureaucrat is what he has done by other people. Thus his best work is someone else's work, for which he takes all or most of the credit. He creates by proxy.

∞ ∞ ∞

One day a senior bureaucrat accidentally left the door to his office open, and he was astonished at the response he drew from his staff. They said he was human, accessible, visible. They praised him as a modern administrator, one who had chosen to place himself in the middle of the action, right in there with his troops, sharing their risks and their worries and their hopes. He wasn't from the old school of administrators, those who demanded dignity, respect and prestige by their very absence, or at least by the rarity of their presence. By hiding themselves behind closed doors. By the distance they kept between themselves and their underlings. By the impression they gave of being above all those people who sweat their lives away on the other side of the rosewood-panelled walls of their offices. No, he was not of the old school, this senior public servant. He was there at his desk, smiling up at anyone who happened to pass his door and look in with surprise, with curiosity, perhaps even with familiarity . . .

"Thank you, sir, for keeping your door open . . ."

"I'm human, too," replies the senior mandarin. "I'm tired of staying all by myself in this empty office, not seeing the pretty secretaries in their light spring dresses, never having a friendly chat with my co-workers. Besides, the air in these new buildings is so bad, I feel I can breathe better like this . . ."

∞ ∞ ∞

The principal and endless task of the senior bureaucrat is to effect a reconciliation between two warring concepts: common sense and bureaucracy.

∞ ∞ ∞

Like nuns who bind their breasts with tightly wrapped strips of cloth in order to underscore their complete separation from the world, to show the strength of their renunciation of life's joys, to symbolize the brutal repression of everything within them that tries to bounce to the surface, so the senior bureaucrat turns his back on life, on his own destiny, represses every thirst and hunger that once, albeit long ago, gnawed at his soul, banishes forever any urge he might have had to laugh or sing, wipes his memory clean of his first hopes and aspirations, those youthful ambitions that used to fire his imagination. Instead, he has chosen to plunge into the great labyrinth that is the Public Service, to lose himself with a kind of masochistic frenzy in its endless corridors, to cover his ears with his hands to block out the siren-songs of all those lost opportunities to do something else, anything else . . .

When common sense is on the verge of prevailing, the senior bureaucrat redoubles his efforts to stop it from triumphing altogether, or at least to delay its victory for as long as possible. His will be a different approach to any particular problem under discussion. Common sense, to him, is not always — indeed is hardly ever — the primary or even peripheral criterion for action.

∞ ∞ ∞

For Descartes, a *tabula rasa* was the beginning of mental activity. To a senior bureaucrat, a clean desk is his day's objective, which he usually achieves during the afternoon toward four o'clock. His *tabula rasa* signals the end, or at least the cessation, of mental activity.

∞ ∞ ∞

When a senior bureaucrat compliments someone, he regards the action in much the same way as he regards his financial portfolio at the stock exchange. If it so happens that a certain investment turns out to be a bad bet, he simply withdraws his money and places it elsewhere, where he hopes it will reap a greater benefit. Similarly, complimenting someone must, in his mind, result in a capital gain to himself; it must pay dividends and show a healthy return on the investment.

∞ ∞ ∞

The senior bureaucrat deals with urgent matters rather than with important matters. Important matters are always postponed until later, while urgent matters spread like a stain, constantly encroaching upon the past and the future, condemning the senior bureaucrat to a life devoted entirely to the ephemeral present.

∞ ∞ ∞

If you suddenly turn over a rotting log, you will catch a brief glimpse of many different kinds of insects scurrying and clambering in all directions: white slugs, lice, centipedes, earth-worms, termites, and so on. The same impression of swarming life can be found in the hidden world of the senior bureaucrat, where each in his own fashion scampers, jostles, hurries, changes places, slithers noiselessly out of sight, makes half-hearted attacks on his neighbour, ducks and feints and parries, disengages himself from one attachment and throws himself into another, moves suddenly, takes a swipe at a passing stranger, lands on his feet, leaps up again, and generally behaves in the manner preordained by his own particular biological imperative. Certainly, all this movement is a sign of life. But how sense-less . . . how repulsive!

∞ ∞ ∞

The senior bureaucrat undertakes to reform an organization in precisely the same way and under the same circumstances that a new disease attacks an organism. It takes a while for the or-ganism to recover from the initial surprise and begin to produce the antibodies necessary for its defence.

∞ ∞ ∞

The mandarin accepts the dismissal by the Minister's office of his plans for the utilization of public lands, which has occu-pied the bulk of his time and energy for the past two years, with a sweet, serene maturity. But he goes berserk if the colour of the new armchair in his office doesn't quite match his drapes, or if someone makes off with his favourite coat-hanger during the lunch hour.

∞ ∞ ∞

Every decision taken carries with it the risk of error. As does every decision not taken. To make decisions is the principal func-tion of the senior mandarin. Or not to make them. He is thus caught between a rock and a hard place. He dreams of a cross between a scapegoat, who would take the responsibility for a bad decision, and a gun dog, who would bring the spoils to the hunter if the decision turned out to be a good one.

∞ ∞ ∞

To a senior bureaucrat, the only bad rule is the rule that wasn't made to be circumvented.

∞ ∞ ∞

It sometimes happens that a senior bureaucrat is in the right for the wrong reasons. Other times, he is in the wrong for the wrong reasons. But most often, he is wrong for very good reasons.

∞ ∞ ∞

The admirable self-sacrifice of the senior bureaucrat, the in-credible drive, those long extra hours that he puts in without pay, the obligation he places on his colleagues and subordinates to stay late with him and to come in on weekends, are often nothing more than his own fear of solitude, his desperate desire to avoid going home alone to an empty apartment from which his wife and children have long since fled.

∞ ∞ ∞

What I detest, says the senior bureaucrat, is getting other people to work. If I do, it's only so that I don't have to work myself. Otherwise, I wouldn't do anything at all . . . Would you like me to run that by you again?

∞ ∞ ∞

Most people think that every problem is to be followed as quickly as possible by a solution. The senior bureaucrat knows full well that that is dangerous thinking, that there are some problems that serve his own best interests only so long as they remain problems, and that they lose their virtue and become useless to him as soon as they are solved. He therefore surrounds himself with a few carefully chosen problems that make him invaluable and further his own ambitions. And he ensures that they remain problems until they have served their purpose. No solution will be found for them until they have ceased to be useful, and show no prospect of being useful again in the future. He is like a pretty woman whom men find enticing as long as she is not pregnant. But once she is pregnant, she becomes much less interesting, or at least she elicits a different kind of interest from them.

∞ ∞ ∞

Conferences, symposia, panels and workshops provide the senior mandarin — that incomparable artiste of management — with opportunities to present a kind of one-man show, a form of dramatic monologue, in order to elicit the adulation of those lesser public employees waiting in the wings. These last will one day rise to the heights themselves, to take their places on the managerial Mount Olympus, to have their turns answering all those admiring questions from an audience of sycophants eager to take the slightest word that drops from their lips as gospel truth. They fling their hands into the air to attract the moderator's attention, they jostle for position at the microphone, they pose — using their best administrative vocabularies, larded here and there with the latest management-seminar buzzwords — high-sounding questions of such exquisite complexity that their sole purpose can only be self-advertisement. Then they return to their seats and look around the room to gauge the effect of their perspicacity on the others, forgetting even to listen to the response, which anyway is full of hesitations and imprecisions, coming from a senior bureaucrat who by now has completely forgotten who asked the question in the first place, and who therefore addresses the entire audience so that everyone present can benefit from the enormity of his wisdom, and marvel at the depth of his penetration.

∞ ∞ ∞

The senior bureaucrat always knows what he's trying to avoid, but often has no idea what he is trying to accomplish.

∞ ∞ ∞

To a senior bureaucrat, justice consists simply in splitting everything down the middle into two equal halves. Any other method invariably drags one into the minefields of logic, proof and counter-argumentation. The fifty-fifty approach, on the other hand, almost always gives satisfactory results. Those defending weak causes are surprised and happy to get so much; those who considered their position unassailable are disappointed, certainly, but usually content to settle for half with their honour intact — which, in a world where honour is assailed daily, is no small compensation. Not to mention the fact that such a solution saves the senior public servant from any debilitating discharge of energy, or even any appreciable mental effort.

∞ ∞ ∞

Every trade and every sport produces a particular, characteristic and stereotypical pose that becomes a sort of international symbol by which a tradesman or an athlete can be easily and quickly identified. For example, the man at his workbench, hunched over his last with hammer raised and ready to strike, is irrefutably a shoemaker. The silhouette of a form crouched low against an invisible wind with a pair of poles tucked under her arms is a skier. Senior bureaucrats also have their typical stance: a man with one foot raised and aimed at the backside of his neighbour, while his own backside is being kicked by the man behind him. In some depictions the foot is replaced by a tongue.

∞ ∞ ∞

Among senior public servants, management almost always deteriorates over time into mere administration.

∞ ∞ ∞

Forced to choose between justice for a subordinate and solidarity with a colleague, the senior bureaucrat opts instinctively for the latter. We must close ranks, he says to himself, to protect ourselves and those like us from the rising tide of reformists of every stamp, especially those who are not like us, who are unknown and without influence. They are making all sorts of demands, applying greater and greater pressure, and even, occasionally, this takes the form of direct assaults on the hierarchical system. We must defend democracy against all these socialists who, if they had their way, would go around making all public servants perfectly equal. Which they are, of course, as are all human beings, but only before the law. They cannot claim equality in the eyes of the senior bureaucrats who make the rules and set government policies. These senior bureaucrats have not only the authority but also the responsibility to put in place as many interpretations, delays and exceptions needed to limit the damage caused by what it pleases you to call equality. I know this sounds confusing and difficult to grasp, but nevertheless . . .

What's that you say? What about justice? Oh yes, we were talking about justice for a subordinate, weren't we? Well, naturally, the ideal would be to have justice for everyone. But justice for everyone is not possible in certain exceptional cases, such as this one. In this particular case there are considerations of a higher nature that I am not at present at liberty to divulge but which are, I assure you, very real . . . But under normal circumstances, yes, certainly. We will have justice. Only . . . not today, not when it's a question of choosing between justice and solidarity with my comrades — er, colleagues. Besides, justice has been abused so often in the past that one more time hardly seems worth bothering one's head about. It's like prostitutes. Someone who rapes a prostitute seems less guilty, somehow, because it's a prostitute's job to have sex with anyone who comes along, and their work often takes them into areas bordering on the illegal anyway . . . What? Of course you're right, all rapists are guilty and must be punished, but some rapists are more guilty than others, that's my point. Raping a prostitute is not so much an act of aggression, as . . . an indiscretion. At any rate, we'll work for justice next time. Let's just forget about it for now — come on, I'll buy you a coffee.

Blind chance serves a senior bureaucrat well by making things work out fifty per cent of the time — a probability he could not hope to achieve on his own.

∞ ∞ ∞

The restructuring of his organization is the route most often taken by the newly appointed senior bureaucrat who wants to draw attention to himself, to stir the imaginations of his new staff, and to impress them with the breadth and depth of his authority. Mostly, though, it is done for the sheer joy of making an arbitrary decision. This is a new — or at least heightened — privilege accorded by his recent promotion, the ability to act on whimsy without fear of reprisal. As long as he stays within reason, of course, and doesn't run the risk of an embarrassing scandal. Considerations of improved efficiency or the well-being of his staff are secondary and purely official justifications (in case he's asked) for the sweeping changes he initiates.

∞ ∞ ∞

The mass production of the metronome posed a serious threat to senior bureaucrats' activities, to their very careers. Fortunately, they succeeded in limiting its use to music.

∞ ∞ ∞

Any decision necessarily entails an element of arbitrariness which an honest decision-maker tries to reduce and circumvent in order to achieve the highest possible level of objectivity, logic and simple justice. The senior bureaucrat, on the contrary, does his utmost to increase the role of the arbitrary in the decision-making process, since it is the only chink through which he can insinuate, like a worm into an apple, his own tastes, preferences and desires. The greater the role of the arbitrary, the more influence he has on events, and the more control he has over his own environment.

∞ ∞ ∞

There are times when, seeing how the top bureaucracy works, one feels a certain sympathy for Nero who, mad though he was, was able to delight at watching Rome burn.

∞ ∞ ∞

The lip service paid to notions of increased productivity and competence by senior bureaucrats is often nothing more than an instinctive strategy to divert attention away from their own lack of productivity and competence. They are like partridges, dragging their wings to lure intruders away from their nests.

∞ ∞ ∞

The senior bureaucrat spends his days on the bureaucratic stage, playing the part that he has learned so well by heart. But when the curtain falls at the end of the matinée, he returns to his more mundane self. He removes his make-up, helps to straighten the chairs in the hall, lights a cigarette, and takes a bus home.

∞ ∞ ∞

As soon as an action gets under way accompanied or even informed by an idea, says the senior bureaucrat, that's when things start to go haywire.

∞ ∞ ∞

What distinguishes a mandarin from an ordinary public servant is that the former understands intuitively that power is attained neither through competence nor through accomplishments, but through inertia and immobility. He knows that doing nothing and letting time slip by is an infallible combination against which all the energy and strategies in the world cannot prevail. It is a force so compelling that it becomes invisible. It attracts neither attention nor even interest, and inspires only lassitude and indifference — the first signs of disintegration and defeat in an enemy. The senior bureaucrat who is obviously doing nothing at all is in the fullest possible possession of his faculties and at the very peak of his ability.

∞ ∞ ∞

Tiny, insignificant events are the senior bureaucrat's daily bread, the sparks that keep his engine firing day after day. Their effect on him is rather as if he had taken chloroform and "speed" at the same time, and they carry him along somewhat jerkily until the office closes at five o'clock. And until he retires at sixty-five.

∞ ∞ ∞

One of the disturbing things about senior bureaucrats is the number and importance of the resources placed at their disposal to enable them to undertake, without let or hindrance, the completely ludicrous and useless projects which they first dream up and then cling to with such demented tenacity.

∞ ∞ ∞

To a senior bureaucrat, the two paths of theory and practice are perpetually parallel: they never join and they never cross.

∞ ∞ ∞

Each morning, the mandarin gives a brisk push to his merry-go-round — following up a remark overheard in the elevator, or making a few phone calls, or arranging a meeting with his directors. This usually suffices to keep the carousel turning all day, and allows him to climb up on the machine himself and to divide his time equally among the various wooden horses which, in time to the music, rise and fall and turn in their concentric circles.

∞ ∞ ∞

At the beginning, the senior bureaucrat aimed higher.

∞ ∞ ∞

The senior public servant slips into the bureaucratic community the way a thief loses himself in a mob. They both know that whatever damage is done will be blamed on the crowd, and not on the individual.

∞ ∞ ∞

You listen to the senior bureaucrat's voice as it runs on and on, dragging out those interminable sentences whose clarity is obscured and dulled not by the import of their words, but by their continual references to himself, some of them articulated, some of them merely implied.

Later, in the building's underground parking garage, you listen to the muffled gurgling of waste water as it passes slowly, slowly, with long pauses and sometimes complete stoppages, through one of those clever, discreet drainpipes that hangs from the concrete ceiling.

∞ ∞ ∞

With senior mandarins, the decision is usually made before there is any argument or discussion concerning it. These last are mere accessories, or accompaniments, which, coming as they do after the fact, serve only to justify and give credibility to the decision itself. They are like walls added to a structure after the roof is in place and functioning quite well on its own.

∞ ∞ ∞

In the Public Service, there are two great but conflicting precepts, which are equally important. The first is always to do everything exactly according to the rules, and the second is always to do the opposite. The great mandarins are those who have succeeded in freeing themselves from the first, and in taking up permanent residence in the second.

∞ ∞ ∞

The Public Service is, in reality, nothing more nor less than a living, autonomous organism made up of a vast number of individual cells. These cells are the senior public servants. What is most curious is that, even if each of these individual cells could attain a high level of complexity and intelligence, the organism of which they are parts would itself remain primitive, instinctive and reactionary. For example, if you jab the organism in one spot, the whole contracts like a muscle that has received a jolt of electrical current. The jabbed cell communicates the shock and a description of its source to its sister cells automatically and at lightning speed, so effectively that the intruder and the nature of his intrusion are known almost instantaneously by every component of the organism, which immediately and in an orderly manner close ranks against the intruder. From that moment on, each cell reacts in exactly the same way to the intruder's presence: it recognizes him, denounces him, and ejects him summarily from the organism.

∞ ∞ ∞

Let us suppose a senior public servant arrives early at his office and works frenetically for the entire day. He is not doing it for the sake of his wife, or his children, or the money — although he certainly won't turn that down. No, he is doing it for himself, for his own personal ambition, or simply because he has a lot of work to catch up on and he can't find anyone to do it for him. He does not pause for a moment to think about his up-coming transfer, or his next holiday, or perhaps his death. These are all questions of a "philosophical" nature about which he knows absolutely nothing, which in fact frighten him, and against which he defends himself by pretending they don't exist. Would you have him work at such a frenetic pace for a public that mocks and misjudges him, or for his faceless superiors who will forget his very name the day after he makes his final departure? He feels the same kind of happiness as a worker in a beehive, who toils away while others keep watch, or make war, or love.

∞ ∞ ∞

Like a crayfish, the senior bureaucrat sometimes seems to be backing up when in fact he is lunging forward. Unlike a crayfish, however, he can sometimes seem to be moving forward when in fact he is falling behind.

∞ ∞ ∞

Suddenly, like the crow in the fable, the mandarin feels worthless, unsatisfied, discontented with himself. How boring work is! How monotonous! He has had enough of this constant decision-making — he wants to think too! So he begins to reflect out loud, just like that, begins so suddenly that his subordinates are dumbstruck, astonished by this sudden interruption, this outburst, this audacity. They are taken completely unawares. Soon, though, when they recover from their initial shock, they begin to come to his aid, to help him through his difficulties as best they can, as they would give quick instructions to a child riding a bicycle for the first time. They supply him with words when he falters and appears to have run out of them; they offer him translations for words that for some reason he can only think of in French; they finish thoughts that he began to expound on but had to give up because the effort proved too much for him; they pretend — while he nods at them amiably — that what he has just said was a masterful and witty summation of what they have all been talking about for the past half hour without being able to come to anything like the perfectly phrased lucidity of their boss. At this the senior bureaucrat smiles, humbly and happily, wiping his brow, lowering his eyes, silencing his admirers with a majesterial wave. What a big happy family they are together! What perfect harmony! What bonhomie, what . . . productivity!

6
Experience

❦

The senior bureaucrat has learned through experience never to get between a dog and his fire hydrant.

∞ ∞ ∞

Pyrrhus was wrong to ignore his counsellor, Cineas, who advised him to rest right away instead of undertaking a series of strenuous military campaigns that would only force him to rest anyway. The senior bureaucrat understands that advice instinctively, with no need for a Cineas.

∞ ∞ ∞

The senior bureaucrat never throws the first stone. But spurred on by another's audacity and supplied with a handy precedent, he always throws the second.

∞ ∞ ∞

Mandarins are like those winged dragons in the picture books of our childhood. Usually, the artists endowed them with ridiculously small, delicate wings that even a child could see could never support such a large and un-aerodynamic beast in the air. They also gave their jaws firebreathing capabilities that never seemed to require refuelling and possessed the miraculous quality of never catching fire themselves. Such improbabilities, however, never seemed to occur to us in those days, and we gladly placed our faith in the dragons.

They haven't changed much since then, these mandarin dragons. We, on the other hand, have grown older and wiser. We know that dragons cannot fly and that the flames they breathe have no power to burn. And we know that, when the fire descends from heaven, it will not come through their mediation.

∞ ∞ ∞

Like King Midas, the great Clerks of State change everything they touch into gold. Their nasty intentions, their shady dealings, their secret deliberations, their most dishonest, not to say their most sordid, activities, when passed through the magic crucible of these new alchemists, are transmuted into generous thoughts, long-thought-out recommendations, and irreproachable virtues. A stranger, unfamiliar with the meandering sinuosities of the Public Service, might see only the smoke and mirrors and take offence at what he supposes to be dark plots, or come to hold these sacred cows in low regard. That's because he is not used to being in the castle, and doesn't know yet how to interpret those midnight creaks on the staircase and cracks in the walls. The old servants, however, know what's what, and smile openly without even lowering their gaze. Somewhere in the house, on a landing or at the end of a darkened hallway, someone is getting the shaft. Figuratively, it goes without saying . . . or does it?

∞ ∞ ∞

Once you become a senior bureaucrat you cannot stop being a bureaucrat until the time comes when you no longer have a choice.

∞ ∞ ∞

If you ever have to choose between a good book and a senior bureaucrat, choose the book. A certain amount of justice and some degree of communication are almost always assured in books, so that you will not feel that you have totally wasted your time. Added to that, you will have avoided the habitual and more or less frequent wrangles that come with any verbal exchange with a senior public servant, and so will have decreased the stress and increased the quality of your life.

∞ ∞ ∞

The senior bureaucrat does not reject all new ideas, only those that are new to him. It is a simple cautionary measure.

∞ ∞ ∞

The mandarin hastens to write his memoirs. Before he forgets them . . . Look, he's scratching his head already . . . Is it amnesia or simply a totally uneventful life that makes his memoirs so difficult to write . . . let alone to read . . . Hello! . . . Anyone there?

∞ ∞ ∞

The senior bureaucrat usually renounces his own point of view when he sees that most of his colleagues already share a common and contrasting opinion on the same subject. He gives up the struggle, preferring to be carried along in the general throng than to be singled out by an opposing view. Partly because it is easier, but mostly because it allows him to identify himself with the majority, say he is no different from anyone else, and be seen to be someone with no rare qualities, original ideas or individualist leanings. If he is going to be wrong, he had better be wrong in the same way as everyone else.

∞ ∞ ∞

The mandarin's greatest strength, and the source of his serenity, lies in his knowledge that no one will believe what is being said about him, even though it is true, because it is so outrageous that people will believe that what is being said is malicious gossip, scandal and lies. He smiles, hidden and safe behind a smokescreen of improbability.

The mandarin understood very early in his career, and it is for this reason alone that he has risen to his present position, that he lives in a world in which appearance is so much more important than reality. The latter is nothing more than raw material in his hands. His job is to take it, shape it, mould it, change its angles and alter its lighting in order to render it more beautiful, more presentable, to give it more colour, than it has in so-called real life. Dull, black-and-white reality stems from the simple, insipid succession of days. Fortunately, however, we have him, the mandarin, the great magician, the master illusionist, who alone knows how to transform the ugliness of things as they are into the beauty of things as they seem to be.

∞ ∞ ∞

When you see a pair of eyes suddenly go out of focus, seem to slip behind a diaphanous veil, pass into a translucent fog, you may be absolutely certain that (unless they belong to the person to whom you are making love) they belong to a senior bureaucrat who is dozing off.

∞ ∞ ∞

The senior bureaucrat knows full well that a good part of reality falls outside the accepted norms, in the margins of the ordinary. That is why he is careful to establish rules and regulations that are not perfectly airtight, but that are on the contrary full of loopholes, escape clauses, contingencies, and exceptions that allow him, if need be, to work outside them, to be able to perform without fear of having to account for his actions or be punished for them. This is very often a useful stratagem. It has exonerated and preserved the reputation of more than one mandarin.

∞ ∞ ∞

Through a peculiar kind of professional transference, which properly speaking has no justification in experience, the senior bureaucrat attributes to other people the same motives he himself would have had in a similar circumstance. So even when the rules don't expressly demand it, he will always ask for a medical certificate from someone returning from sick leave, suspecting him of having taken off from work for some other reason.

∞ ∞ ∞

The experienced senior bureaucrat is the one who can tell you in advance exactly why and how a certain undertaking hasn't a snowball's chance in Hell of being successful. He's been there so often himself he feels perfectly at home with failure.

∞ ∞ ∞

When senior public servants retire, they often continue to hang around outside their former offices to relive old times and to share their memories with the younger generation. Half forgotten, they get in the way, they drape themselves in a faded dignity, proud of all the laughable but inconsequential episodes that form the bulk of their insignificant careers. They are waiting for senility or death to erase forever the painful throbbing of their past, a past without substance or depth, without meaning . . . It must be like looking at a face that you detest, and which is your own.

∞ ∞ ∞

In most human beings, age and experience lead to greater wisdom. In senior bureaucrats, they lead to greater mistrust.

∞ ∞ ∞

It may happen that a senior bureaucrat will one day say something to you with so much charm, gaiety and spriteliness, will leave you feeling so warm and sympathetic, that it will be quite some time before you realize that his actual words have been nothing more than the usual idiocy.

∞ ∞ ∞

Being a senior bureaucrat is an incurable and irreversible condition. No matter what he does, Mr. Hyde will never be Dr. Jekyll again.

∞ ∞ ∞

Once in a blue moon, through a curious combination of chance, patronage and error, it happens that a subordinate is propelled suddenly into the senior ranks of the Public Service without having had time to prepare himself for the shock of transition, or to familiarize himself with the new duties which he knows nothing of and which will drive him into pretense from the first day onward. He takes on a bewildered air, he walks uncertainly, staggering like a gladiator suddenly released from a dark cage into a brilliantly lit arena where thousands of expectant eyes wait for him to begin battling a ferocious but as yet invisible beast.

∞ ∞ ∞

As the old song says, everybody wants to go to heaven but nobody wants to die, so the senior bureaucrat looks passionately forward to retiring but becomes more and more terrified as the day approaches. Never having learned how to live for himself, he views his new-found freedom as a menace. What a burden it is to have to think up things to do with one's time. What torture to have to set one's own goals. What anguish for a thing of vapour to see the disappearance of its container.

∞ ∞ ∞

When a senior bureaucrat errs, what consoles him, what gives him his revenge over those who know that his black is actually white, is the knowledge that the system will never force him to correct his mistake, will never require him to rectify his error, and that it is he who, by default, will be seen to have been correct.

∞ ∞ ∞

When you have said everything you wanted to say to a senior mandarin, you have said far too much.

∞ ∞ ∞

If a senior bureaucrat offers you a gift at night, do not thank him until you have examined it carefully by day.

∞ ∞ ∞

Progressing from experience to wisdom in a senior bureaucrat means progressing from a full run to a dead march, from dead slow to full stop, from paralysis to coma.

∞ ∞ ∞

When you have said or written something against a mandarin that subsequently seems to you to be unfair and even malicious, and you regret having allowed yourself to go to such extremes, and then you watch your would-be victim in action, you are invariably surprised by how much your version has fallen short of reality. What astonishes you is not that you have tainted the honour and the reputation of a senior bureaucrat, but rather that your attempt to do so has been so ineffectual, so insufficient, and that you have proven yourself to be too naive to know to what depths of dishonesty, betrayal and cheating a senior bureaucrat will sink. The truth — you see it now so clearly — is always worse than the feeble fictions of your imagination, measured by the ridiculous scale of your pinched morality, or far, far too strong for the poor little darts you have blown at it that have since occasioned you such unnecessary scruples.

∞ ∞ ∞

Senior bureaucrats are to ordinary people what almanacs are to real books.

∞ ∞ ∞

We must consider senior bureaucrats with the same air of detachment with which we watch those magnificent grosbeaks at the end of a long winter. They come to our feeders, eat up all the sunflower seeds, and take off without the least show of gratitude. They leave us with nothing but the pleasure of having watched them in action.

∞ ∞ ∞

A senior public servant will often resolve a problem by pretending he hasn't noticed it. He understands that when a solution is either nonexistent, or inapplicable, or works to his own disadvantage, then the simple passage of time is an excellent substitute. Left for a sufficient amount of time, the problem worries away at itself, diminishes, shrinks, and finally disappears altogether. In some cases, it is even possible to take credit for having solved it, thus turning what at first looked like a defeat into a resounding victory.

∞ ∞ ∞

The senior bureaucrat is a strange warrior: he uses his shield to guard his back rather than his chest.

∞ ∞ ∞

At first, the senior bureaucrat is a bundle of passions. Gradually, the urge to get ahead smothers these passions one by one until, just before he retires, they are completely dead.

∞ ∞ ∞

The senior bureaucrat has known all along that the opposite side of any question can also be true. Or false. Depending . . .

∞ ∞ ∞

On his death-bed, seized by a sudden fit of lucidity, the senior bureaucrat declares: The difficulty is not dying. It is dying without having done anything worthwhile, after having had the illusion of the opposite for so long.

∞ ∞ ∞

The best remedies against senior bureaucrats are space and time. Or both together, if possible. Take yourself as far away from them as possible, and if it is absolutely necessary for you to come into contact with them, make it seldom and swift.

∞ ∞ ∞

To a senior bureaucrat, the race is always over, the goal has always been reached, and the die has been cast.

∞ ∞ ∞

In a senior bureaucrat, experience overtakes and eventually replaces what has been learned. Put another way, what the senior public servant knows he has learned almost exclusively from what he has experienced, rather than from the more usual exercise of any intellectual faculties.

∞ ∞ ∞

When senior mandarins repeat the same falsehood often enough and over a long enough period of time, it becomes the truth.

∞ ∞ ∞

For the senior bureaucrat, injustices are like toxic substances: if they are contained, if there are no visible or detectable leaks, or if no one is aware of their presence or their danger, then he is content to let the situation go on indefinitely, without settling on any means of either hastening or delaying its progress. But if things get out of hand, if the situation begins to resemble a major oil spill, if the public seems about to become indignant, or above all if his own career seems likely to suffer, then he will mete out justice swiftly and generously.

7.
Politicians

Mandarins have the same success in offering resistance to politicians as bronze statues in public parks have with respect to pigeons. It goes without saying, some minor annoyances are unavoidable.

∞ ∞ ∞

The difference between a politician and a senior bureaucrat is this: the former, using money he receives from willing contributors, as a result of huge advertising campaigns, strives to accomplish great projects that will bring him much personal gain, whereas the latter, using money he receives from unwitting contributors who pay their taxes, strives to accomplish small projects that will bring him much personal gain.

∞ ∞ ∞

The mandarin is secretly thrilled, although he cannot show it openly by smiling because he is constrained — it goes with the job — to exercise, or to appear to exercise, perfect control over his emotions at all times and with every gesture. But there, right in front of him, lying face-up on his Brazilian rosewood desk, is the note he has just received from upstairs: 2-BS. His seat number at the next First Ministers' Conference. After weeks of intense lobbying and strenuous negotiating, mostly by his secretary, with the insolent gnomes and trolls who work at the Prime

Minister's Office, here is his victory! He is to be seated in the first row of seats reserved for special guests of the government, right in the centre of the room, quite separate from his colleagues — those who were invited at all — who are placed in the second and even third rows. Best of all, 2-BS is almost directly behind the chair of the Prime Minister himself, which means he'll be precisely in the field of vision of the TV cameras, they'll be trained on him — er, on them, of course — most of the time. Oh yes, no doubt about it, this is a great, great triumph. He will be seen across the nation, his younger subordinates will point him out with admiration and respect, journalists will have to find out who he is, his family will recognize him and burst with pride at the honour he is doing them, even the ministers will notice him and, perhaps, remember him at an opportune time — provided, of course, that they're not annoyed at having the limelight stolen by a non-elected official . . . 2-BS. He couldn't have hoped for a better seat. For the three solid hours that the meeting lasts he'll be a water-lily shining on dark water. After which he'll go back to being a frog.

∞ ∞ ∞

In the belief that his Minister is totally lacking in intelligence, education and experience — as sometimes happens with the elected — but is nonetheless the people's choice, the senior bureaucrat puts forward six different strategies for attaining a certain objective. Five of these are totally unrealistic, impossible, even foolhardy, especially the third, which is suicidal. The sixth, however, is plausible and defensible, and is the one favoured by the senior public servant himself, who has often had recourse to this classic subterfuge in order to impose his own choice on those higher up. The Minister is cornered and led to adopt the desired solution, but feels he has made the decision himself.

It sometimes happens, however, that the clever bureaucrat is hoisted with his own petard. The Minister, suspicious of the mandarin's logical tyranny and fearful of the determinist prison into which he wishes to cast him, leaps over the trap without so much as touching it, upsets the senior bureaucrat's carefully set plans and, head lowered, chooses the third option, the worst of the lot.

∞ ∞ ∞

Just as municipalities, in their public gardens, place sidewalks where they wish the public to walk rather than where the public walks in reality, so the government in power does what it likes without taking the slightest notice of public opinion, because it works on the assumption that the people are wrong. Or rather, it assumes that the people are well intentioned but uninformed and too inclined to believe in old wives' tales. It therefore allocates a certain portion of public funds to a kind of secret publicity program—all above-board and accounted for, of course — the end of which is to gently persuade the populace to walk where it has placed the bloody sidewalks. Statistics show that two out of every three people polled begin to think along the desired lines in less than a month. And it only costs the taxpayers a few dollars each to have their minds changed.

∞ ∞ ∞

The mandarin, at public expense, has his volumes of rules and regulations rebound in red to match his new rosewood bookshelves. How ridiculous, he says, that they should have been originally bound in green. Green isn't even the colour of a political party likely to form a government. Publishers have no political savvy, nor enough common sense to establish and nurture warm and lasting relationships with those who hold the reins of power.

∞ ∞ ∞

In a democracy, the wisdom of the people is far greater than that of their politicians, no matter how determined politicians are to have them believe otherwise. The only exception to this general rule is in the lack of wisdom shown by the people when they choose their politicians. In such cases, even a politician would do better, because if it were up to him rather than up to the people, he certainly would choose someone else.

∞ ∞ ∞

The senior bureaucrat force-feeds his Minister in much the same way as the French force-feed their geese. Every day, without respite, he stuffs him with reams and reams of paper typed single-spaced. The result, admittedly, is not pâté de foie gras, but something better: a Minister so busy reading that he has no time to interfere with the work carried out by his senior mandarins.

∞ ∞ ∞

The senior bureaucrat thinks he's really in the know when his Minister lets him in on his hidden agendas, important strategies or even state secrets. The senior bureaucrat is wrong. The truth is that the Minister knows that he can use the bureaucrat to release certain official information without having to go through official channels of communication. He knows the senior bureaucrat is fervently adept at passing around ordinary, anonymous, manila envelopes — those famous plain brown packages of the professional informer.

∞ ∞ ∞

They make a good couple: politicians have the privilege of making idiotic promises, and senior bureaucrats have the pleasure of carrying them out.

∞ ∞ ∞

Senior mandarins are masters of non-verbal complicity. They have perfected the art of turning a blind eye at the proper moment, especially when the matter concerns one of their own masters, the politicians, who always have some little thing to keep quiet about and who are constantly being exposed to the ferreting and malevolence of journalists, those vultures without a grain of mercy or pardon . . . It may seem ridiculous, but the simple act of not seeing something, or of seeming to not see something, can pay some very interesting dividends — usually in the form of advancement — for the attainment of which the senior bureaucrat is more than willing to not see just about anything. So long, of course, as the politicians understand that he has in fact seen what he has not seen, and that they appreciate the importance of discreetly rewarding the not-seeing of it without of course having to ask him what it is he has not seen. Senior bureaucrats can feign this blindness with such aplomb that not even the truly sightless can hold a candle to them.

∞ ∞ ∞

Politicians have a tendency to think and do whatever the voting public wants them to think and do. Senior bureaucrats have a tendency to think and do just the opposite, a luxury they can easily afford since their duration does not depend upon regular elections.

8
Subordinates

Senior bureaucrats talk so convincingly about their high standards and, occasionally, provide evidence of them with such pomp and circumstance that one ends up wishing one had just taken their word for it in the first place. Their subordinates are not fooled, however. They can smile behind their hands or turn a yawn into an enthusiastic nod with the best of them. But they hold their peace. Either because they are looking forward to the job they want, or are looking out for the job they have.

∞ ∞ ∞

Like mistresses and courtesans of former days, who were integral parts of the court and even accompanied the king on his travels, so the senior bureaucrat's secretary and closest employees over the years become unconditional admirers and guard dogs of their chief, and follow him with their files and paraphernalia each time a promotion or other career mutation takes him to a new office, a new building, or a new department. They arrive as one, they invade, they occupy, they spread out, they install themselves, they reign.

On the other hand, if the senior bureaucrat is suddenly seized by the mysterious and nearly always fatal malady called disfavour, his coterie and often even his secretary must also share his fate. And when the ultimate moment of demotion comes, followed by leave of absence, followed by actual dismissal, his band leaves with him. Administratively, they even cease to exist. As in some ancient cultures certain tribal members are buried with the deceased chieftain: his wives, his mistresses, even his servants.

∞ ∞ ∞

The annual performance appraisal of regular public servants is a miraculous invention of the senior bureaucrats. It provides them, under cover of the most impeccable legitimacy, with an extremely subtle instrument for either blackmail or vengeance, permits them to shorten a particularly recalcitrant subordinate's leash, and, on occasion, generates considerable advantages on the side. Such as an interesting article written by an underling but signed by the senior bureaucrat, or a few tabs picked up at a good restaurant by an eager assistant, and even, with a bit of luck, an amorous rendezvous, quick but so invigorating, over the lunch hour.

∞ ∞ ∞

If there is a difference of opinion between a subordinate and a mandarin, the subordinate keeps quiet for fear of being right.

∞ ∞ ∞

Senior bureaucrats are such sensitive creatures. They cover their ears when they hear the horrible screams of the people whose throats they have cut and who don't have enough sense to die quietly. Figuratively speaking, of course. All murders committed by senior bureaucrats are figurative, which is why they seem so unreal.

∞ ∞ ∞

The senior bureaucrat carefully and discreetly separates out from his entourage anyone who shines with a particularly brilliant light, for fear that the comparison with himself will not be favourable. And also to eliminate any future competition.

∞ ∞ ∞

If, contrary to his usual custom, a senior bureaucrat smiles at you, it is because he has momentarily mistaken you for a colleague of superior rank. Disabuse him at your own risk.

∞ ∞ ∞

Admittedly he is no Einstein. But he is ambitious. He works like a madman. He arrives at the office hours ahead of everyone else, and at night the fluorescent light in his office is on long after everyone else has gone home. In the eyes of the night watchman, with whom he is on a first-name basis and from whom he cadges cigarettes, and the cleaning staff, who wet-mop the long, silent corridors of the government office buildings every night, he is a demon for work. Bent over his desk, his face red with concentration and real sweat dripping from his brow, he writes down the words and figures that the next day he will submit to his boss's boss, who has taken him under his wing and told the man's immediate superior that he has never had a subordinate so devoted to his duty, so productive, so eager to impress his superiors . . . And while the big boss reads the work he has done so diligently the night before, the hard-working subordinate waits patiently, his face a study in worry, supplication and good will, for the single word of appreciation he hopes will be tossed his way. In the end, like the faithful and obedient dog he is, he goes back to work, not knowing any better way to pass the time. Oh work, your talons are sharp!

∞ ∞ ∞

A subordinate can admire a senior bureaucrat, but not for anything would he have him for a friend, or a relative.

∞ ∞ ∞

The senior bureaucrat does not trust that new employee who gets along well with everyone, does his work conscientiously, and who places dedication and honesty ahead of pleasing his superiors and doing their every bidding. He is a dangerous element, and deserves close watching.

The senior bureaucrat is pleased with the ingenious but simple strategy he has developed, which works extremely well when he wants to get rid of someone he has judged to be undesirable. No major fracas, of course. It must be done discreetly. Over the medium to long term. Long enough to make it difficult to establish a causal link between the subordinate's downfall and the circumstances that brought him to it.

First, he gives his future victim all the rope he could possibly want: he reduces his work load, gives him every holiday and day off he asks for, encourages him to take time to think, engages him in long, rambling discussions about current or past policies, leaves him alone for long periods, sometimes for whole days at a time, doesn't invite him to certain meetings under the pretext that he would find them boring or a waste of time, never asks him to account for anything, leaves him pretty much to himself, without pressure or deadlines or responsibilities.

Thus administered, the treatment is painless but nonetheless devastating in its effect. And although it takes time to produce the desired results, it is irreversible and has no known antidote. Gradually, the subordinate, apparently so coddled and privileged, begins to lose his way in the organization, has no direction, no reason for being there that anyone can put their finger on. As the months go by, as his participation diminishes, his motivation evaporates. Eventually his symptoms turn into downright complaints, into a definite illness. He begins to show signs of withdrawal, he feels abandoned, deserted, ostracized, isolated, forgotten. What is most peculiar is that he himself is hardly aware of the state he is in. He exhibits a sort of euphoria that prevents him from noticing the profound transformations that he is undergoing . . . Until the time when he finds himself in a kind of race, or contest, or competition in which he has to measure himself against other people. Then he is like the rabbit who sees, too late, the turtle crossing the finish line: he suddenly realizes he is no longer fit for battle, that his inactivity has made him unable to compete, that his knowledge and experience are no longer keeping pace with those of his colleagues; in short, he understands that one day he simply stopped growing, perhaps forever. And it was the day when, smiling and mysterious, his boss encouraged him to take it easy.

The mandarin has taught his bulldog docility, obedience and submissiveness; his subordinates as well. If not, castration, or even amputation, may await them.

∞ ∞ ∞

Some senior bureaucrats are basically opposed to having employees at all, because they represent a check to the free rein of their capricious will. But they put up with those who are protected by a union or association, or those whose grievances are known to a large number of sympathetic colleagues.

If, on the other hand, the subordinate is a member of no fraternity or syndicate, is somehow isolated and exhibits other forms of vulnerability, if his disagreement with the upper bureaucracy is not public knowledge and is unlikely ever to be so, and if his cause is of no interest to a large number of people, then the senior bureaucrat will quietly crush that subordinate under his heel with all the weight at his command. As a smiling child will calmly squeeze a helpless bird to death in his closed fist.

∞ ∞ ∞

There are in nature certain instinctive understandings between animals of different species. There are parasites, for example, that accompany, assist, or clean up a host of a much bigger size — those little birds, say, that ride around on the backs of large mammals — in exchange for food or protection or simply transportation. Similarly, in the Public Service, there exist strange and improbable pairings based on mutual personal interest. Each member of these duos supports and assists the other, the weaker one serving, backing up and favouring the stronger, and the stronger carrying the weaker along with him in his wake, tossing him the occasional promotion and generally protecting him from being ambushed by other citizens of the swamp.

∞ ∞ ∞

When a senior bureaucrat fires someone from his organization, he doesn't necessarily inform the person. For all practical purposes, he no longer exists. This situation can go on for years.

The senior bureaucrat wants to see incompetence flourish in someone he wishes to get rid of and encourages it with a strange solicitude, as one would rub dirt into — or at least neglect to wash out — a wound so that it will become infected.

∞ ∞ ∞

The senior bureaucrat needs subordinates around him so that he will look important by comparison, to others as well as to himself. When he is alone, his importance falls into some uncertainty. His greatest strength is the weakness and submissiveness of others.

∞ ∞ ∞

To a senior bureaucrat, it is inconceivable that right and reason might be on the side of a subordinate. If you show him irrefutable proof that such is the case, he will feel betrayed by some divine power, so convinced is he that right and reason belong to him alone.

∞ ∞ ∞

The senior bureaucrat feels a sort of admiration for the subordinate whom he otherwise despises, whose throat he has just slit — figuratively speaking, of course — and who is now dying without a murmur of protest, who is in fact displaying nothing but a mild detachment, a commendable indifference, a bold stoicism of which the senior public servant himself would be incapable. He will watch in fascination as the subordinate slowly and quietly gives up his life's blood, dying a kind of hero's death.

∞ ∞ ∞

When you find yourself witnessing an exchange in which a subordinate is telling a senior bureaucrat what he actually thinks of him, observe the subordinate carefully: you'll probably never see him again. In the Public Service, frankness is almost always an error in judgement.

When competitions are held, the senior bureaucrat awards the job to the subordinate whom he knows is capable of anything, who will balk at no perversity, underhandedness or fabrication to achieve his ends. He needs someone like that on his team, someone to whom without a word spoken he can entrust the baser tasks that he could never undertake himself for fear of being placed in a compromising position . . . Nothing out of the ordinary in this: merit should be rewarded in those who carry out orders faultlessly and without a qualm. In fact, the Devil himself is competent; if he weren't, he would not be able to do evil efficiently, and that would place him dangerously close to God.

∞ ∞ ∞

One's opinion of senior bureaucrats improves considerably at the end of office hours, on payday, when the sun is shining, and it's the beginning of a long weekend.

∞ ∞ ∞

A senior bureaucrat without subordinates is inconceivable. The two go together like a solid body and its shadow. If, through some cruel quirk of fate, a mandarin loses all his underlings, he will spend hours on end, day after day, in search of them, like a ewe bleating inconsolably for her lost lambs. If he cannot find them anywhere, he will do whatever he can to replace them with new ones — seconding the lowliest secretary who does not belong to any one boss, the most unsuspecting junior officer who meanders down his corridor, or even one of his friends whom he can draw into his lair and whom he will unflinchingly sacrifice to his hierarchical hunger.

∞ ∞ ∞

Junior public servants can choose between the Scylla of rules and regulations, and the Charybdis of the senior bureaucrats' despotic whimsy.

∞ ∞ ∞

The senior bureaucrat is instinctively suspicious of the subordinate who has no need of his salary to live on. Such an employee is like a bucket without a handle, or a drawer without a pull; he is hard to get hold of, difficult to push or pull in the desired direction.

∞ ∞ ∞

The senior mandarin has no need of a philosopher among his employees. He doesn't want subordinates who are right, he wants subordinates who agree with him. The last thing he needs is an employee who can think for himself, or even at all.

∞ ∞ ∞

The mandarin looks upon his subordinates as pawns to be moved, instruments to be played upon, marionettes whose strings he alone can pull. All his attention is concentrated on the game, not on the individuals, who are anyway replaceable and interchangeable. As a great general sees a whole army on the move rather than individual soldiers marching.

∞ ∞ ∞

A successful senior bureaucrat is often the one who has found a subordinate competent enough to do his work for him, and diplomatic or discreet or servile enough not to claim credit for it.

∞ ∞ ∞

The senior bureaucrat has known all along that, in a hierarchy, subordinates who are right too often end up dying of starvation. At the very least, their careers suffer from acute horizontalism. It is important to be wrong often enough to keep one's job and ensure an ascending trajectory. At any rate, the distinction between being right and being wrong is an extremely subtle one, and doesn't make much difference anyway, as the senior bureaucrat has also always known. Why place oneself and one's career in mortal jeopardy for such a trifling thing? He has taken for his motto the old saying: It's better to be a live chicken than a dead duck.

9
Tactics

When a senior bureaucrat gives you the official explanation for something, you can be sure that it is incomplete, inaccurate or even downright false. To a senior public servant, the unofficial is always closer to the truth.

∞ ∞ ∞

When confronted by a hurdle, the first instinct in a senior bureaucrat is to deny its existence. His second is to do nothing. His third is to get around it. The fourth is to go away and come back later. If he is absolutely forced to confront the obstacle, he will. But he'll go under it.

∞ ∞ ∞

The senior mandarin has an instinctive dislike of dictaphones, tape recorders, videocameras, still cameras, photographic equipment in general, in fact recording devices of any kind that brutally preserve what is said or done, leaving no room for interpretation, nuance, memory lapses, reasonable doubt, negotiation or diplomacy . . . Such apparatus place good faith and reputation in the gravest danger because they leave no door open for an honourable retreat in case of emergency, and bring to violent and dangerous light actions or words that were undertaken originally under the protection of confidence and secrecy.

If a certain senior bureaucrat greets you in a friendly manner, you're finished. Somewhere, at some time, you have let down your guard.

∞ ∞ ∞

As a dog, faced with a loathsome toad, instinctively knows that he cannot attack it with impunity, the senior bureaucrat hesitates before pouncing; he looks left and right, he circles the creature in an attempt to hide his intentions, he ascertains whether or not it is protected by a guardian angel, a godfather, an influential father-in-law, a secret friend, even a politician, any personage who could conceivably come to its defence. If he determines that his prey might prove dangerous because of alliances it has made, he will withdraw his claws, hide his fangs, and smile contritely and even with obsequiousness. But if he satisfies himself that his victim is powerless and has no connections to worry about, he leaps on it like a wolf on a lamb — figuratively speaking, of course, as are all the movements of a senior bureaucrat — and, taking advantage of his prey's inexperience, weakness, inattention or, should he be so lucky, blindness, he will flip him over and trample him. In the name of merit or some other convenient principle.

∞ ∞ ∞

Rivalries, manoeuvrings, the locking of horns, these are for senior bureaucrats nothing more than means of maintaining contact, of keeping lines of communication open, of interacting with one another. It may seem as though they are divisive elements, that they create adversarial positions by pitting one senior bureaucrat against another, but they don't. The truth is, they bring them closer together, they unite them, they weave them into a tight fabric. Rivalry plays the same role in the bureaucracy as sex does in the life of the praying mantis.

∞ ∞ ∞

The senior bureaucrat has such a high opinion of his own incompetence that he never hesitates to use it as a lever with his superiors. He threatens not to retire, for example, unless his separation package is vastly improved.

∞ ∞ ∞

If a senior bureaucrat helps you out, do not misread his motives . . . In helping you, he is helping himself. It is even likely that he is profiting more than you are from the aid he is giving to you. As the sum of mass and energy in the universe is a constant, so the senior bureaucrat never loses in any transaction, no matter what he does. For him, giving is just another form of receiving.

∞ ∞ ∞

The senior bureaucrat will gladly do without love if he can get to fornication without it.

∞ ∞ ∞

The senior mandarin flees merriment and spontaneity, avoids word-play and even suppresses smiles. He trains his throat to emit only serious, guttural sounds and consciously slows down his own body's natural rhythms. The idea is to create an illusion of perspective, of light and shadow, of depth, of which his own thin presence, without this constant effort, is incapable.

∞ ∞ ∞

The senior bureaucrat knows that people will believe anything if you whisper it into their ear, and he makes the most of it.

∞ ∞ ∞

The senior bureaucrat knows that neither the Church nor the State can punish indecision and confusion. So he indulges fully.

∞ ∞ ∞

Senior bureaucrats charged with the task of carrying out the restrictive cut-backs decreed by the government always apply them most assiduously — to their great regret, of course — to their colleagues and, above all, to their subordinates, no matter how much damage those policies may do. Jobs must be lost, salaries must be slashed. But it is extremely rare that these same cut-backs are applied with the same rigour to the senior bureaucrats themselves. Through some mysterious means, the official, discreet and subtle criteria by which these things are judged always manage to exclude the people whose job it is to apply them. But this is not surprising. Gross incompetence aside, have you ever heard of an executioner being beheaded by his own axe?

∞ ∞ ∞

About one thing the senior bureaucrat is adamant: don't wait for posterity to prove you right. Be right now.

∞ ∞ ∞

In the Public Service, being different breeds intolerance, and eventually animosity. The degree to which you are detested is directly proportional to the degree to which you are different. Your chances of being detested are lowered, however, if you affirm your difference in important matters rather than in small things. This is because the larger issues will only make your listener yawn, whereas the tiny, insignificant things are those that are closest to his heart. Novice bureaucrats take heed: disagree violently over what interpretation should be given to certain government policies, but be infinitely more circumspect when it comes to office supplies.

∞ ∞ ∞

With the same sincerity and sadness shown by Mafia bosses at the funerals of those they have ordered assassinated, a senior mandarin will be all solicitude and compassion with those whom he has executed (again, figuratively speaking), will arrange to have someone else (the Minister, the government) or simply the circumstances (the economic situation, bad luck) blamed for a decision reached by him alone, most often for purely personal reasons, usually known only to himself. He knows full well that a guilty person showing remorse is already half pardoned, at least in his own eyes.

∞ ∞ ∞

The senior bureaucrat makes important decisions without a moment's hesitation. Not because he is particularly good at them, but because he knows he probably won't be there if the consequences prove to be disastrous.

∞ ∞ ∞

To the senior bureaucrat, democracy, which is essentially a system that expresses the preferences of the greatest number of people, is the worst of all possible political doctrines, at least from an individual point of view. He knows very well that ever since his childhood he has been losing the games he plays with disconcerting regularity, that more and more people are claiming their right to come and take away his marbles. That the common and vulgar of the world have just as much chance to succeed as do people of quality. In order for him to grow, to flourish, to triumph, he needs a protected environment, where his progress depends entirely on the will of one person, or at least on a very select group of people. He needs time to mould them to fit his own special requirements, to soften them and condition them, to coddle and coax them. He needs time, too, to ensure that holding official competitions for promotions, for example, would be a waste of time, that all possible rivals would already have been eliminated, that all rules and regulations would already have been bent in his favour, that his appointment to the post would be a mere official confirmation of an already existing reality, an administrative formality the only practical purpose of which would be to draw more attention to his own meteoric rise in position and substantial increase in salary.

∞ ∞ ∞

The senior bureaucrat assiduously perpetuates the myth that he is above suspicion in all things, just as women of the most ancient profession will defend their virtue and honour with a delightfully surprising vigour, at least until the opening negotiations.

∞ ∞ ∞

When a senior bureaucrat suddenly and without provocation attacks someone who has done nothing to him, it is meant merely to take advantage of the element of surprise and to strike the first blow without risk to himself. The legendary gunfighters of the old American West used the same tactic.

∞ ∞ ∞

There is nothing worse than a senior bureaucrat with insomnia. At least normal bureaucrats sleep seven hours a day.

∞ ∞ ∞

There were a few moments when he thought that the game was up, that this time he had gone too far, but now the senior bureaucrat is breathing more easily. The naive but honest young man who has just left his office was coerced into making two solemn promises: one, that he will never divulge to anyone the circumstances of his resignation; and two, that the victim — we might as well call a spade a spade — will never for whatever reason seek redress from the State. What a happy coincidence that, in exonerating the State, the senior public servant is also exonerating himself, and that in protecting the interests of his country, he is at the same time serving his own ends . . .

∞ ∞ ∞

The senior bureaucrat understands perfectly well that in not acting he runs the risk of committing an error. But he also knows that by acting he runs the same or perhaps even a greater risk of making a mistake, and that he would be attracting attention to

himself to boot. Is this a dilemma? Not at all . . . The senior bureaucrat simply rejects both alternatives in favour of a third,
which is to put the whole problem off indefinitely, at the same
time invoking sufficiently plausible and convincing reasons for
doing so that no one would ever dream of accusing him of lacking
initiative or strength of character or a decisive nature. The ideal
manager, in his mind, is the one who knows how to bide his time
and do nothing that will lessen other people's confidence in and
opinion of himself.

∞ ∞ ∞

The senior bureaucrat is a past master in the art of letting
someone else run the risk in a potentially hazardous endeavour.
If the project succeeds, however, he will be the first to take credit
both for facing up to the danger and for bringing the matter to
a successful conclusion.

∞ ∞ ∞

The senior bureaucrat knows full well the market value of a
secret. Not its monetary value, which is usually negligible, but
its worth as a bargaining chip, which can sometimes be very
interesting.

∞ ∞ ∞

If ever you receive an official memo from a senior bureaucrat
explaining, clarifying or justifying a particular governmental
policy or decision, ignore the scribbles in black ink on the white
paper and hold the document up at arm's length against a strong
light. There will always be more truth in the watermark.

∞ ∞ ∞

As a stratagem, a senior bureaucrat will often continue to
speak or write long after he has run out of things to say, simply
to make his adversary believe that he has even more powerful

arguments in reserve. The tactic frequently succeeds. The enemy falls asleep.

∞ ∞ ∞

The old senior bureaucrat still prefers sleeping to working. As long as he can be sure he'll wake up.

∞ ∞ ∞

The senior bureaucrat did yesterday what he should have left for tomorrow so that tomorrow he can do what he should have done today. Which is why he is doing nothing today.

∞ ∞ ∞

A senior bureaucrat who starts by shaking your hand will often end up shaking you by the throat. When that happens, you can forestall his next move by covering your more sensitive parts.

∞ ∞ ∞

The mandarin knows that justice delivered too late is really a new justice. He also knows that most people don't see that as an abuse of justice; those who do see it and complain about it are comfortingly rare. This is because most people suppose that slow progress through aeons of time is a disagreeable but natural attribute of the machines of justice, like the greening of vegetation or the salting of the ocean. That is why procrastination, slothfulness, forgetfulness, inaction and retardation are the preferred weapons of the senior bureaucrat. They are effortless and painless. Such weapons go a long way toward resolving, painlessly and effortlessly, problems so numerous and thorny that the senior bureaucrat could otherwise only resolve them by doggedly battling with them, calling upon all the energy and enthusiasm he is capable of.

∞ ∞ ∞

It does not bother a senior bureaucrat that he is reviled and detested as long as, in the long run, he achieves his desired goal, which may well be that people love and respect him.

∞ ∞ ∞

Sometimes a senior bureaucrat will exhibit a cold, implacable logic when financially punishing, as often and as long as he feels is necessary, a subordinate with whom he has had a disagreement. This goes on until the subordinate, weakened and impoverished, falls into line with the senior bureaucrat before becoming bankrupt altogether. The latter savours his triumph, congratulating himself on his convincing tactics, his rigorous rationalism, and his powers of persuasion. He has exercised his absolute right, like a soldier in combat whose duty is to destroy the enemy in the most effective manner possible, even if it means shooting him in the back.

∞ ∞ ∞

Staff cut-backs as decreed by the government of the day, usually to shore up its popularity with voters by handing over to them living, human and anonymous victims, furnishes the senior bureaucrat with an unexpected opportunity to rid himself of subordinates he has wanted to sack for a long time but whom he could find no legal or excusable reason for firing. As in barbaric armies of long ago, in which the old and the wounded were put to the sword in times of famine or when the rest had to move quickly, the senior bureaucrat, under cover of a perfect legitimacy and without incurring the slightest risk to himself, inflicts his silent and triumphant reprisals on those he wishes to be rid of. Or else he sits back calmly and watches the small and the feeble perish at someone else's hand, perhaps delivering a private eulogy at their wake. They are modern cannon-fodder.

But at the same time, profiting from the general confusion and acting against the grain, he helps out a colleague who has been placed in personal danger by the government's exceptional measures. The colleague then owes him a favour, a debt of honour that the senior bureaucrat will cherish in his heart, and will call in at a later time. At the right time and place. At an opportune moment.

∞ ∞ ∞

The best way to deal with a problem, says the senior bureaucrat, is to pretend that it has already been dealt with, or that it simply doesn't exist, and to act accordingly. It's amazing how many people you can fool this way. Not to mention that it saves you a great deal of time and considerable labour. Why deal with a problem when it is far more advantageous to ignore it or deny that it's a problem?

∞ ∞ ∞

When under attack in the press, especially in the newspapers, mandarins call upon the best writer among them to be their champion and to defend the honour of the clan. They pass him new information, unpublished documents, otherwise inaccessible files prepared by their own staff, anything that will help him compose a convincing, vibrant, sincere refutation of the charges made in the article. The refutation is published in the same newspaper that carried the allegations, and will avenge the insult suffered by the entire tribe. All at government expense, of course, since it was the government, after all, that had been attacked.

∞ ∞ ∞

The senior bureaucrat is careful not to find solutions. Finding a solution is tantamount to solving the problem, and what would happen to him then?

∞ ∞ ∞

Beware . . . When a senior bureaucrat gestures for you to lean over so that he can whisper something in your ear, he is really going to spit in your ear. Figuratively speaking, of course . . . What? You thought I meant literally . . .?

To die must be terribly tiresome. For the opportunistic senior bureaucrat, however, it is a once-in-a-lifetime chance to escape the routine.

∞ ∞ ∞

The cleverest senior bureaucrats know that in their world virtues such as justice, honesty and charity circulate extremely slowly. Their own actions, therefore, proceed swiftly, and before the consequences become clarified they are off seeking new horizons, covering their tracks, obliterating their past, erasing their names. They get the new experiences and the lucrative promotions. Others are left behind to raise the feeble offspring of their administrative copulations.

∞ ∞ ∞

When a senior bureaucrat laughs, it is not humour he sees, but profit.

∞ ∞ ∞

The senior bureaucrat chooses those times to work when he is being watched.

∞ ∞ ∞

Be careful! Never take your eyes off a senior bureaucrat who is not looking your way. He is certainly up to something.

∞ ∞ ∞

Beware of the senior bureaucrat who smiles at you when something has gone wrong. You may be the one he intends to blame.

∞ ∞ ∞

The mandarin flees instinctively from brightly lit places and seeks out the shadows, feeling more comfortable in the damp half-light that favours secret manoeuvres, buries their traces, and confounds witnesses.

∞ ∞ ∞

Assured of impunity and anonymity, the senior bureaucrat strikes out valiantly.

∞ ∞ ∞

Great politicians come and go. Top bureaucrats are with us forever. Knowing that, they sit down and wait.

∞ ∞ ∞

Before agreeing to play musical chairs, the senior bureaucrat always makes sure there are as many chairs as there are players. It is his unwavering rule never to run risks when he can achieve his goals by other means.

∞ ∞ ∞

The senior bureaucrat loves things that are haphazard, accidental, discontinuous, interrupted, broken, or patched, in short, everything that can prevent an investigating committee from going over past records to trace something back to him, from following the stream back to its source, from travelling back along the chain of cause and effect to the original cause, to catch the senior public servant red-handed. He therefore spends a great deal of his time cutting Ariadne's thread into tiny bits and scattering them to the four winds, in his effort to outwit all the bounty hunters who are trying to track him down with the intent of exposing him when he least expects it.

∞ ∞ ∞

"Tonight, it's just no good. All your laborious and damaging theories about mandarins have come crashing down around you. You see them collapsing before your very eyes, or rather ears.

You have just heard a senior bureaucrat stand up before a conference room full of people and, in a loud, clear voice, speak extremely well of someone you thought was his sworn enemy. Everyone in the room has heard him and can bear witness to his greatness of spirit, his generosity, magnanimity and compassion. How can you go on vilifying this man, heaping scorn and ridicule on his saintly personage?"

"You are hopelessly naive. You haven't understood anything that is going on around you. Between this senior bureaucrat and his enemy, war and peace are being waged simultaneously. One knows that if he attacks the other publicly, he runs the risk of doing more damage to himself and his cause than to his enemy. He tries so hard to say such good things about his rival only so that others will form a higher opinion of him. Such a weapon could prove decisive against his adversary, who must now feel himself drowned, smothered and defeated by the deployment of an unexpected amount of good will and gentleness, and who will be unable to swing civil opinion back to his side . . .

All in all, this is nothing but shadow play: when the day is over and the witnesses have gone home, the battle will resume with renewed vigour, no holds barred — not even the knee to the groin. No doubt about it, your grasp of the rules regulating the games of the mandarins is very shaky indeed."

∞ ∞ ∞

A dog warns you *before* he bites. A senior bureaucrat after.

∞ ∞ ∞

The senior bureaucrat will go to any lengths — almost to the point of telling the truth — if it means getting himself out of trouble, or a colleague into it.

∞ ∞ ∞

If a senior bureaucrat arrives early for a meeting, it is so that he can have time to choose a seat, without seeming to, that places him in full view of whoever is chairing the meeting, while giving the other participants the best view of him, ensures that his back is to the bright light coming through the window, and generally assures him of a dominating position at the table. In this way he seeks to compensate for the weak personality and lack of presence with which nature has endowed him.

∞ ∞ ∞

Since the senior bureaucrat's permanent intention is to pull one over on you, you can forget about ever pulling one over on him. He has had vastly more experience at it, has been bred and groomed for it, and there is nothing about it he can learn from you that he doesn't already know and hasn't already done a hundred times over. You can accuse a senior public servant of many faults, but he is no sucker.

∞ ∞ ∞

When a senior bureaucrat asks for your advice, he is playing a very cruel game with you. If you can guess his own preference, and advise him loudly and clearly to do precisely what he has every intention of doing anyway, you win. If you can't, you lose. He will then be in a position to call your sense of judgement into question. And he will do so.

∞ ∞ ∞

Never count on the sincerity of a senior bureaucrat. It is like one of those plaster eggs one puts in a hen's nest in order to induce her to lay real ones.

∞ ∞ ∞

The senior bureaucrat loves to shroud the status of his new staff members in a cloak of mystery and uncertainty. He does this by postponing indefinitely the exact date on which they are to be definitely integrated into his organization, and by pushing into the unforeseeable future the application of those boring and complicated rules that confer upon them their automatic rights as public employees. Rights like the one that protects them from the dictates and caprices of his own absolute will, for example. Rights that are difficult for him to contravene without risking damage to his integrity as a senior bureaucrat.

The amazing thing about a probationary status of indefinite length is the beneficial, nearly miraculous, effect it has on the employee. It endows him with a beautiful suppleness, an infinite malleability, a blind and smiling obedience that a pronounced sense of security would shatter in a moment. Probationary status preserves in an employee a sense of virginal newness, the charm of a fresh conquest, the spirit of a pioneer. It softens and conditions him and disposes him toward acquiescence, like a piece of meat that has been marinated overnight in a bowl of red wine.

∞ ∞ ∞

The senior bureaucrat has the true gifts of a magician. Only when he has succeeded in directing your attention elsewhere does he perform his best tricks.

∞ ∞ ∞

The senior bureaucrat has an acute sense of impartiality and fairness. His time and energy are distributed with absolute equality among his many deficiencies.

∞ ∞ ∞

When a senior bureaucrat finds it impossible to actually hide certain pieces of important information, he will try to slow down their distribution so as to give himself a comfortable lead over those who also wish to make use of them. In this way, he will be seen as having been the first to hear the news, and consequently will look good. In addition, in this race to not tell a thing, he may be able to find room for some rapid manoeuvring that will permit him to realize a small personal gain without too much effort. As in the stock exchange, or at the track, where one can make a small fortune if one can obtain a reliable tip early enough.

∞ ∞ ∞

When a senior bureaucrat becomes interested in you, when he participates in your joys and weeps at your sorrows, when he asks you about your problems and shares your woes, it is likely that he smells some sort of profit for himself.

∞ ∞ ∞

The opinions of senior bureaucrats on just about all things are supple and changeable, portable and easily dismantled. They are chameleons; they can change to any colour to blend into the background.

∞ ∞ ∞

When a senior bureaucrat, for no apparent reason, does you a favour, ask yourself very, very seriously whether or not you can afford such a luxury.

∞ ∞ ∞

A mandarin always dissembles. It is second nature to him, a ceaseless obsession, a sort of unending chess game the purpose of which is always the same: to make believe. Reality becomes diffuse, diaphanous and, eventually, superfluous.

∞ ∞ ∞

When a senior bureaucrat changes the subject in the middle of a conversation, it is not always craftiness or guile: often it is simply that he has forgotten what he was talking about.

∞ ∞ ∞

When he makes a mistake, when he is in error, or simply when he thinks he is, the senior bureaucrat is not above eating humble pie. He will place his neck invitingly on the block. He will beat his chest. He will expiate his guilt. In public. Ostentatiously, so that no one can miss it. So that everyone will say:

"How admirable! What courage! What a gesture! Who can blame him now?"

In short, what mastery he has over himself, others and even events; he comes out of the situation unscathed, cleansed, stronger and more esteemed than ever before. Thus the senior public servant benefits most from his worst mistakes.

∞ ∞ ∞

Wherever you are — in church, boarding an airplane, visiting a fine restaurant, attending a ministerial conference, the opening of a new office, a wine-and-cheese party, a Minister's Christmas party, looking for a parking space, anywhere, anywhere at all — it seems that the senior bureaucrat has managed to get there ahead of you, to be actually seated right in front of you. Unless it's a funeral. Or when it's a function meant to underscore his own importance or celebrate his dignity, in which case he follows the official protocol that requires him to be late. Which requires everyone else to wait for him.

∞ ∞ ∞

The mandarin excels at not speaking the truth without actually lying, at withholding evidence without denying it exists, and at not acting without seeming to do nothing. If he leaves behind him few real successes, it must also be said that little remains of his passing that can be brought against him.

∞ ∞ ∞

The senior bureaucrat is willing to make any accommodations, exhibit any amount of flexibility, or participate in any compromise. He puts so much water in his wine, in fact, that he is in far more danger of drowning than he is of getting drunk.

∞ ∞ ∞

Knowing that happiness engenders happiness and sadness leads to sadness, the senior bureaucrat, who is usually sad and uneasy, occasionally assumes an air of gaiety in the presence of others in the hope of fooling them as well as himself about his true nature. Like a hunter putting decoys in a pond, he hopes that through the imitation he will attract the real.

∞ ∞ ∞

One half of a senior bureaucrat is engaged in spying on the other half.

∞ ∞ ∞

Habit is so deeply ingrained that the senior bureaucrat instinctively hides what everyone else already knows perfectly well.

∞ ∞ ∞

When a senior bureaucrat makes an obvious mistake during a conversation, give him a little slack, in the hope that he will come back to the truth on his own. If you try to prove him wrong and force him to admit his mistake, he will become annoyed and resist most forcefully. He will refuse to admit that he has made a mistake, even at the risk of hurting himself or his cause. It's like fishing for salmon or bass: if you pull too hard on the line, you'll tear the hook out of his mouth and lose him forever.

∞ ∞ ∞

Laughter, among the mandarinate, has a strategic function. It has nothing to do with gaiety. If, however, a senior bureaucrat does express gaiety, it can become a sign of weakness, a momentary lapse, a straying from the rule that dictates that he must not laugh, engage in word-play or simply enjoy himself. If he does, he will endanger his current status and his chances for promotion. The more he laughs, the lower his ceiling is. Unless, of course, the laughter is strategic.

∞ ∞ ∞

When a senior bureaucrat provides you with one or even several excellent reasons for hiring or not hiring a given person, he does so for other reasons, which themselves are hidden. His motivation is almost always elsewhere.

∞ ∞ ∞

A senior public servant who tames an animal does so with the intention of eating it.

∞ ∞ ∞

As squirrels gather nuts in autumn in readiness for the rigours of winter, a senior bureaucrat collects personal letters, handwritten notes, confidential reports, unofficial accounts of conversations, scraps of paper of all sorts. Through the years they accumulate, following events, naturally, with no particular effort. They have no immediate use; they may never have any. But you never know. One day, a disagreement with a colleague, a mishap, a compromising mistake or an incriminating circumstance may put him in the difficult position of having to defend himself against some accusation or other. This way, he is prepared. His arsenal will be at the ready if a compromise is to be negotiated, a friendly solution to be arrived at, a discreet bit of blackmail to be carried out, counter-charges to be brought against his accuser, or even if an old rival is to be brought down with him.

∞ ∞ ∞

Would you like to consign a mandarin to silence? Congratulate him for a brilliant action he did not take part in. He will allow the mistake to go on as long as possible.

∞ ∞ ∞

Some senior bureaucrats are like money-losing gold mines that stay in operation only through government grants, for the lack or poor quality of the ore prevents them from ever being profitable. To produce a single bar of the pure yellow metal, tons and tons of slag must be processed. Oddly enough, mandarins themselves are aware of the problem which, in their view, arises from the insufficiency and limitations of their colleagues. To solve the problem, they bring in consultants recruited from the private sector, reputed for their fast, punctual, efficient execution of any project. Of course, these nationally renowned specialists enhance the credibility of the results in the eyes of the mandarinate, even in the eyes of those who were unable to carry out that very project.

∞ ∞ ∞

When a senior bureaucrat performs some official function, his laughter is almost always a type of falsehood. It does not arise from a comic situation, or from natural gaiety. It speaks of his desire to both please and deceive. Or of his desire to cover up the true reasons for his laughter.

∞ ∞ ∞

Senior bureaucrats sometimes sound like horoscopes. Sufficiently vague to be applied to anyone and any situation, while giving the impression of referring to a specific person or situation. If we find nothing there for ourselves, or recognize no familiar signs, we simply decide that the prophecy was meant for someone else, or another situation we know nothing about. Today, we conclude, the gods have nothing to say to us . . . Perhaps tomorrow, it will be our turn. And we go about our business, without ever questioning the validity of the oracle.

∞ ∞ ∞

Given his predilection for ready-made thoughts, suitable for believing in, and the vertigo he feels when faced with the challenge of a blank sheet of paper, the senior bureaucrat commits large-scale plagiary. He feels no remorse. If he does reveal his sources, it isn't out of intellectual honesty. He is only showing you how thorough his research was, and adding weight and authority to his point of view.

∞ ∞ ∞

The senior bureaucrat will refuse to commit to paper a verbal promise he's made you. Not because that might cast doubt on the worthiness of his word or his honour. But because a written promise might not lend itself, at some later date, when you want him to fulfill it, to the different interpretations he might want to give it, to take into account not only changing circumstances and new imperatives, but also his explanations and justifications for his refusal to keep it.

∞ ∞ ∞

Divide and conquer . . . The senior bureaucrat smiles and offers no resistance, flattered at being credited with an age-old tactic that assumes he possesses great intelligence, uncommon ambition, and an innate sense of strategy. Of course, he never intended to divide and conquer; he is not up to such a worthy transgression . . . But it's always pleasant to have a legend to one's credit . . .

∞ ∞ ∞

Here is how to avenge yourself against a mandarin who is full of himself and incompetent at the same time. In hundreds of little ways, cause him to have a lofty opinion of his own valour and efficiency, make him believe that his colleagues have extraordinary esteem for him. His vanity will want to believe you, and he will act accordingly. The result: he will appear ridiculous in everyone's eyes. Besides, who knows . . . Given the confident, tenacious smile he is already wearing, someone else may have dreamed up the same stratagem, and recently put it to work.

∞ ∞ ∞

Have you done a favour for a mandarin? He will express his gratitude, of course. Less to thank you for the service already rendered than to elicit another for himself. Either directly from you, or from others who might witness his gratitude and be better disposed to do him a similar good turn in the future.

∞ ∞ ∞

When a woman agrees to make love, often she is only yielding to the strength, hold and impulse of a man of her acquaintance who is already astride her anyway, and not because she feels any passion for him. Besides, resisting might cause an unpleasant scene that could compromise her relations with him, and even stain her reputation as an honourable woman in the minds of eventual witnesses.

In the same way, when a senior bureaucrat surrenders to the arguments of a powerful colleague and humbly accepts his advice, the victory is due less to the common sense and logic of the colleague, and more to his position, power and rank. Not that the senior bureaucrat's intelligence, reasoning and the whole sad parade of his virtues are weak and without effect; they must yield to that which they have no chance of successfully resisting. Besides, if he did resist, he would create an uproar that would attract attention to the poor mandarin and compromise his immediate security and future promotion.

It is much better, says the senior bureaucrat, to get it in the ear today than to get it in the back tomorrow.

∞ ∞ ∞

To get a horse's attention, show it oats. Whistle if you're dealing with a dog. Use a stick if it's a donkey. But if you find yourself with a senior bureaucrat, talk to him about himself.

∞ ∞ ∞

Why should the senior bureaucrat work to get his promotion when he can earn it simply by playing bad tennis with his superior?

If you are in pain, the senior public servant will display sympathy. Less out of compassion than to avoid the charge of being indifferent to human suffering. He submits himself to a convention that procures him no immediate benefit, but that he must respect. Otherwise, he will drop in public esteem and, in the long term, his situation and career may suffer. You see, his official motivation is rarely his real or true one; the hidden reason is the correct one. Or, more likely, the one hiding behind the one hiding behind the official one.

As for your pain, you know where you can stick it . . .

∞ ∞ ∞

You are happy. You are free. You have finally gotten him off your back, or at least you think so. In any case, you left him, you are no longer part of his entourage, his ministry, his bureaucratic universe. You even changed city, province, country. Weeks, months, even years have elapsed since you last saw him. You have banished the very name of that mandarin from your memory.

But it's no use. At a turning point in your new career, when you want to change jobs or seek promotion, during a phone conversation to solicit the mandarin's opinion about you, he will loom up again, with or without your knowledge, with his latent memories, his blind prejudice, his faulty judgement; he catches you from behind, he's upon you in the wink of an eye and, in his grave, serious, falsely sympathetic voice, under the cover of serene objectivity, he flagellates you from a distance, he tears you apart with a smile, and in the mind of this stranger, your eventual employer, a time bomb is set ticking that will explode and ruin the opinion he is forming of you.

Your mistake was thinking you were free. Despite time and distance, an abstract but very real string kept you securely tied to him. As if a fisherman put a hook in a fish he had already caught and threw it back into the water, not to return it to its element, but to extend his pleasure at making a catch in the deep, dark water. And while the fish believes its momentary loss of freedom is over, while it's still alive and desperately trying not to die, the fisherman takes his pleasure at its expense. After which, weary or blasé, he will reel it into the boat one last time and gut it without a second thought.

∞ ∞ ∞

Over the years, the senior public servant has learned that the best way to overcome an adversary is to have the perseverance to hate him long enough.

∞ ∞ ∞

When it comes to tactics, the mandarin prefers conspiracy to assault. The former is not only less dangerous; it demands no courage.

∞ ∞ ∞

In the mandarinate, danger catches up to a victim from behind. It rarely confronts him head-on.

∞ ∞ ∞

Normally, society judges, sentences and executes. The senior bureaucrat reverses the traditional order. He sentences and executes first, to increase his chances of obtaining a favourable judgement later. The method is efficient, for few people are inclined to defend those who have already been subject to the opprobrium of sentencing or the finality of execution.

∞ ∞ ∞

Do you wish to attract or influence a mandarin? Avoid the trap of idealism, nobility, angelic conduct. Instead, learn to play upon his cupidity, falseness, evil intent, concealment, mediocrity . . . Your success will be measured by your ability to skillfully use the worst in him.

∞ ∞ ∞

We know of a senior bureaucrat who doesn't seek the praise of others. He prefers the safety of doing it himself. In front of you. Without blushing. The way a deviant masturbates in public.

∞ ∞ ∞

A member of the mandarinate who confesses does so because he cannot cover up the scandal any longer. He wants to share in the honour of having uncovered the truth, even if it is at his own expense, as a way of controlling it and manoeuvring it into the best position for himself.

∞ ∞ ∞

Senior public servants are the speed bumps of any organization.

∞ ∞ ∞

Definition of a recommendation: when a mandarin who cannot do something praises one of his bureaucratic friends who cannot do it either, in order to convince others that both can do it.

∞ ∞ ∞

Whatever the circumstance, the senior bureaucrat sees silence as the least dangerous position.

∞ ∞ ∞

The mandarin may seek reconciliation for a hundred different reasons. But they all have one thing in common: they arise from plotting and tactics.

∞ ∞ ∞

A senior bureaucrat's words reveal more by what they don't say than by what they do say. What he says ostensibly conceals what he isn't saying and attracts attention to the gap. You have no trouble finding out what is not being mentioned, which, in fact, constitutes the true subject of the conversation.

∞ ∞ ∞

Rival bureaucracies have been known to play the most outrageous, immature practical jokes on each other. The classic trick, of course, is when one bureaucracy pretends to jealously guard and protect a top mandarin whom it has been trying unsuccessfully to get rid of for years. It manages to arouse the covetous interest of another bureaucracy which, naive or badly informed, falls into the trap, honestly believing it has gotten its hands on an administrator of the first order. It obtains him at an exorbitant price, certain it has struck a genuine and decisive blow against its adversary. It doesn't take long to discover, however, as the crafty trader chortles with laughter, that the horse is blind, toothless and lame.

10
Rivals

Instinct and experience have taught the senior bureaucrat that, in his office, in restaurants, in waiting rooms, any place where his counterparts gather, he should always sit with his back to the wall.

∞ ∞ ∞

When, in the heat of discussion with a mandarin, you seem to be right, that is when you are most wrong.

∞ ∞ ∞

A senior bureaucrat of our acquaintance always eats alone. Just as a predator creates a space around itself and drives away the animals upon which it feeds.

∞ ∞ ∞

If I don't get along with him, says the senior bureaucrat, it's because we have the same opinion of each other.

∞ ∞ ∞

This mandarin detests you with such level-headed dignity that you are almost flattered, even honoured to have attracted such a magnificent enemy.

Two mandarins have their knives out. But don't expect raised voices, hurtful words or hostile faces. Their mutual hatred takes on the appearance of serenity, balance and reason. Any departure from their normal behaviour would betray a momentary loss of control, proving the fallibility in an apparently faultless facade, tacitly admitting a lack of maturity, an involuntary confession of weakening self-confidence, the beginning of the enemy's final victory . . . The contempt they feel for one another finds expression in correct, proper language, in terms strictly within the limits of good taste. But in this implacable and relentless struggle, these two hate and harm each other with a skill and ease unattainable by us common mortals. In fact, the man in the street could not even detect the movements of these fleeting minds, for everything occurs at too subtle a level. Just as the human ear cannot sense certain high-pitched sounds which can be detected by dogs.

Anyone who does claim to have detected hatred between two mandarins will be subject to the most severe censure, then treated to a strange spectacle, in which the protagonists, better to demolish his theory, will make a public display of affection, fervent friendship, amused complicity and good humour. You see, rivalry, disagreement and discord are not admitted into the lofty spheres in which these grand creatures dwell. Were one of our two mandarins to take it into his head to transgress this unwritten law, his irrevocable downfall would quickly occur, ensuring his adversary's victory — an unthinkable proposition.

It is even possible, in an effort to preserve this illusion of harmony, that the feigned friendship of one adversary for another will become a true one, or at least change into a sort of ambiguous, temporary feeling made up mostly of respect for the power, tenacity and viciousness of the other opponent. In fact, friendship among the mandarinate is often nothing more than overheated rivalry brought to a fever pitch. Living, persistent and superbly mastered hatred.

∞ ∞ ∞

When a senior bureaucrat learns that a friend, a colleague or a rival has been promoted, he hastens to telephone him, or write a short letter of congratulations. To remind the other that he exists. Better to conceal his resentment at not having been chosen. To demonstrate his strength, his impassiveness, his equanimity in the face of a bad roll of the dice. To renew a friendship which — if Lady Luck had smiled on him, and not on his friend — he would have probably let waste away. So that the increased influence of his rival might one day, at the opportune moment, serve his own ambition, which remains intact, despite this temporary but humiliating setback.

∞ ∞ ∞

Just as a soldier without a target is unhappy and incomplete, lacking an enemy to help define himself, the senior bureaucrat joins his colleagues and finds himself in rivalry, opposition and struggle. Whatever you may think, they are as good a social cement as friendship, cooperation and fellowship. Through them, the mandarin finds a goal to pursue, an objective to reach, a meaning to his life.

∞ ∞ ∞

When the senior bureaucrat does not know something, he instinctively pretends he does, but only after checking that his colleague doesn't know either. If — against all odds — his colleague does know, or at least pretends to know, then our bureaucrat resigns himself to telling the truth, or at least what is absolutely necessary to tell, though he suspects his colleague of lying, and not knowing either. But a suspicion without proof remains just a suspicion. How can he get the cat out of the bag? After all, maybe his colleague really is telling the truth, in which case our suffering bureaucrat would be mortified to be shown up, especially in public . . . When all is said and done, the best liar wins, which is a form of justice.

∞ ∞ ∞

Among the mandarinate, there is no greater pleasure — indeed, it is a passion — than to correct, modify or criticize someone else's working copy.

The senior bureaucrat regards his colleagues with suspicion, knowing they have definite and irrevocable opinions about him that he can do nothing about, knowing also that he will never know what they are. But he finds consolation in sharing with these same colleagues — except for the one in question — the same secret opinions about each of them.

∞ ∞ ∞

Senior mandarins are the largest antibodies known to man. They oppose — discreetly, of course — campaigns hatched by newly elected governments to bring "new blood" into the mandarinate, a pretext for importing friends from the private sector to whom favours are owed. The reason? Their undying fear that some hairbrain might accept the invitation and create some tough competition. Fortunately, this does not happen very often. But when it does, the mandarinate is well positioned and on the alert. They need little time to neutralize the intruder and spirit away his corpse. Figuratively, of course.

∞ ∞ ∞

When planning out his strategy, the efficient mandarin makes careful allowance for the influence exercised on his project by the dishonesty and treachery of his colleagues, in the same way that he takes into account his deadlines, budget, personnel requirements, alternate solutions, etc. He even incorporates these variables into his planning, neutralizing them and transforming them into positive factors. For example, he knows the moment to disclose a false secret to one of his colleagues, to give the latter time to discreetly inform an adversary, so the adversary can react in a certain predictable way . . .

Better than anyone, the effective mandarin can predict the form and time of the inevitable betrayal, since he himself would follow much the same path under similar circumstances. He has long been accustomed to this regime, just as a miner learns to breathe and function two kilometres below the ground.

∞ ∞ ∞

A senior bureaucrat always has his best scars on his back.

∞ ∞ ∞

A mandarin we know would never kick an enemy when he's down. For fear of aggravating his chronic backache when he bends over.

∞ ∞ ∞

Nothing is sadder and more moving than the death of a mandarin. Contrary to public opinion, he does indeed die. Or rather, he is put to death. Somewhere, in the unctuous silence and the subdued lighting of a governmental penthouse, behind the fake marble and reflecting windows of the mighty tower, there is a click, barely audible, immaterial, close to the ethereal. Someone makes an apparently banal remark, someone smiles delicately, someone refrains from saying something he could say. And suddenly the world of the senior bureaucrat is turned upside down, and the hunter becomes the prey. He is judged and sentenced in absentia. But nothing is apparent yet. Even he is not aware of the sentence. In fact, he will never know, he will always be ignorant of the cause of his own death.

First, the telephone stops ringing. A few hours later, the senior bureaucrat begins to notice; the telephone on his desk becomes a foreign presence. After a few days, he is positively edgy about it. During that same week, a fellow senior bureaucrat cancels lunch at the last moment. At the beginning of the following week, the secretariat neglects to send him the agenda for the weekly management committee meeting which, that day, began an hour earlier. The mandarin feels that something is amiss. His nerves tingle. Why has the phone stopped ringing? Why are his calls returned when his callers know he isn't there?

Little by little, the clues add up; silence and stillness take up permanent residence. And so, after a few weeks of this regime, the mandarin loses his direction, his pole, his balance. He floats round and round on a lake that is circular, flat, stagnant. He shouts, but no one hears, or wants to hear. He waves his arms, but the people on the shore are blind. He won't give up: as hours stretch into days, he strives to understand these absences, this silence. He persists with the dogged determination of a caged animal that paces back and forth, left and right, tirelessly, instinctively, blindly, the length of the solid enclosure that separates it from the forest.

Then, one day, by accident, he learns of his forthcoming resignation, from a stray memo, a rumour heard by his secretary, at the end of an eavesdropped conversation between two underlings. He leaps to his feet, he protests, he argues, he struggles, he promises, he begs. All in vain. When he sees the issue is hopeless, he surrenders to his fate, with the grotesque thrashings of a half-slaughtered steer.

The other mandarins, impassive spectators, pat themselves on the back. The shunning and execution have run their course without incident.

∞ ∞ ∞

If, during a meeting, a senior bureaucrat sees he is about to take his rival's side, he will press his lips tightly together. He would rather grasp at any other viewpoint, no matter what logic and common sense dictate, even if he has to defend a ridiculous position.

∞ ∞ ∞

The senior bureaucrat who cannot prevent a rival from earning the esteem of others consoles himself by thinking that, at least, he will never win his. Yet he can't help realizing just how illusory and ineffective his ill will is, since his rival has no idea it even exists, so puny is his grudge.

∞ ∞ ∞

I endeavour, says the virtuous senior bureaucrat, never to wish a premature death on my boss, whom I would still love to replace, to finally become the boss of all bosses. But the devil is a tyrant, and I am not always successful. Time moves so slowly in this kingdom. Change takes too long. I pray that God will intervene, that a divine and deadly accident may occur, perhaps terminal cancer or, if not a quick heart attack, at least a new case of AIDS.

∞ ∞ ∞

In general, the senior bureaucrat will not speak well of a colleague or even a rival without first making sure that his words will reach the appropriate ears. So that the person receiving the praise knows he is indebted. So he will feel morally obliged, in return, to pay back this debt of honour in a way he sees fit. After all, these exchanges of favours help improve the social environment, increase productivity, create a positive climate for good relations among those people whose only ambition is to serve the interests of the nation.

∞ ∞ ∞

The senior public servant will pretend to fall into the trap set by a colleague if, by doing so, he can lure this colleague into a second trap that he himself has prepared, whose jaws will clamp shut at some later date. Merely a game, you say? If you like. But it can be a fatal one, at least as far as careers are concerned.

∞ ∞ ∞

Have you noticed this mandarin, praising the enemy he has only just defeated? The display is designed to prove and illustrate his own worth for having vanquished his adversary.

∞ ∞ ∞

A senior public servant driving to work in the morning displays reflexes that have been acquired over years of bureaucratic warfare. He skillfully manoeuvres his car so that no other vehicle can slip in between him and the one in front of him. Even if it means risking an accident. Purely for the pleasure of arriving at the intersection first. To hamper the intruder and force him to stay back. To confirm his primacy and priority. To never yield. To be obstructive.

∞ ∞ ∞

This senior bureaucrat, everyone knows, is a fool and an incompetent. But his colleagues will never tell him that outright because of his rank and power, and especially because of their own rank. No matter how mediocre it is, they still cling to it. The senior public servant will spend the rest of his working life in ignorance of what others think of him, and of the fact that their opinion is certainly justified. He will die without ever having known, an innocent victim of this ignoble conspiracy against him.

∞ ∞ ∞

What is most irritating about a senior bureaucrat successfully cheating an adversary is not so much the trickery itself, which can be accepted if necessary, but the fact that the mandarin thinks he's more intelligent and sly than his rival. It's more important for him to think himself clever — about which he has doubts — than to think himself powerful — about which he is certain.

∞ ∞ ∞

The senior bureaucrat knows that if he is able to impress on his colleagues the idea that his rival suffers from some sort of handicap, he can rest easy: victory is assured. When people have the notion of a handicap hammered into them through frequent, insistent repetition, the idea germinates in their minds like a beautiful root of mandrake, slowly filling with poison. The senior public servant is aided by a cruel and instinctive human inclination, which is to ignore and shun and isolate, if possible, all those who suffer from a physical, psychological or intellectual handicap.

He must first sell the idea, for example, that his rival is susceptible to mood swings, or that he talks excessively and impulsively, that he has a tendency to crack jokes, that his health is not all that good, his physique not imposing enough, that he is already on the other side of middle age, he has had no experience in the private sector, his wife left him for another man, he was seen in an art gallery, he has obvious union sympathies, he buys his suits at discount department stores, etc. Pick any of these handicaps, as mild as they might be, and with a minimum of care and feeding and the proper repetition, any one of them can send out roots, grow and snuff out the host's reputation in his colleagues' minds. The process is irreversible, the rival never recovers, and triumph is complete.

∞ ∞ ∞

When, in mockery, a mandarin imitates a rival's words and bearing, that's when he is most typically himself.

∞ ∞ ∞

Senior public servants carry out a simple yet terrible vengeance on their critics and detractors. They observe the strictest silence toward them, whatever they say or do, crushing and pulverizing them under the weight of their contempt. This tactic is most effective. It is also convenient, for it requires no mental effort. An excellent cost-benefit ratio.

∞ ∞ ∞

The mandarin sees his career as a long session in a billiard parlour. There, he embarks on an interminable game of snooker where it is just as important or more important to prevent his rival from making a good shot as it is to score points himself. The winner is often the one who prevents the other from displaying the full measure of his talent, even if he is not particularly good at the game.

∞ ∞ ∞

When a senior bureaucrat witnesses the disgrace and fall of a colleague, he expresses his regrets. He seems to be truly pained;

he displays all the exterior signs of sadness and compassion. Except for that little smile that he can't quite wipe off his lips.

∞ ∞ ∞

There are mandarins who fancy themselves intelligent and skillful and who, by design, feign mediocrity and incompetence to better fool their adversaries. This strategy usually works since the others are completely taken in, and never can distinguish between what is fake and what is natural.

∞ ∞ ∞

The senior public servant always shows more respect for his rivals and enemies than for his underlings.

∞ ∞ ∞

We know of a senior bureaucrat who, to hide his true jealousy, makes a show of being jealous of a moderately successful colleague.

∞ ∞ ∞

If he is unsure of his superior's support, the mandarin will treat his adversary with kid gloves. He hesitates, delays, makes concessions, negotiates the best possible solution. But if he is assured of support from above, he rushes in, imposes his will, jostles, upsets, rams the business through.

∞ ∞ ∞

When, at long last, a senior bureaucrat has the opportunity to judge and sentence his adversary, he apes to perfection a magistrate who is truly regretful at having to decide against the defendant on some difficult question, but who must do so, despite himself, in the name of duty and justice.

∞ ∞ ∞

The danger that threatens a mandarin more often comes from his allies than from his adversaries. It also springs from behind, rather than looming up ahead.

∞ ∞ ∞

Just as the great predators of Africa choose their prey among the weak and elderly in the herd, the senior bureaucrat who wants to attack someone waits for the moment when his intended victim is in difficulty, for example, when he is bereaved or in failing health. Experience has taught him that the chances for success are better then.

∞ ∞ ∞

When he hides the truth from a rival or adversary, when he tells an outright lie, speaks ill of him or slanders him, or deceives him or others about him, the senior public servant quietly pats himself on the back for his talents as master of tactics, a negotiator and diplomat.

∞ ∞ ∞

The senior bureaucrat fights his adversaries not so much with hatred as with contempt.

∞ ∞ ∞

If, in the heat of debate with a senior public servant, you have the last word, it may well be the last one you will ever have with him.

∞ ∞ ∞

The mandarins who are blind in one eye blithely mock those who are fully sighted.

∞ ∞ ∞

The senior bureaucrat displays good taste and moderation in his contempt for you. And so you are indebted to him, and he rises in your esteem.

∞ ∞ ∞

When a colleague is in distress, rather than lending a helping hand, the mandarin will often apply a swift kick. If possible, in complete anonymity, in case fortune turns and the colleague becomes a man to be reckoned with, one with a powerful memory to boot . . .

∞ ∞ ∞

The senior bureaucrat generally fears any threat emanating from the mind, especially humour, the only acid strong enough to penetrate his thick skin. His fear of this is particularly strong, for humour is one weapon he cannot handle and use to any effect, given the apparent complexity of its design and its incompatibility with his profession and status. Otherwise, his position is secure, all drawbridges have been raised, the barbarians safely outside.

11
Benefits

The senior bureaucrat has no trouble displaying honesty and loyalty in small matters. Not only is his reputation improved, but his self-esteem rises as well. Dishonesty and disloyalty come to the fore in important matters only, when the benefits are really worth the effort. At times like these, he will overcome the pain and displeasure at being disapproved of by others, and disappointed with himself.

∞ ∞ ∞

For the senior public servant, a secret is simply a piece of information to be divulged at some later date, when the memory of the oath of silence and confidentiality has all but faded away. This suits him perfectly well, since it falls to him to choose the moment when the revelation will have the most impact and yield the greatest returns.

∞ ∞ ∞

The mandarin remains impassive when his master the politician, caught red-handed at some inadmissible commerce, uses him as his scapegoat. When reporters fill their columns with rumours of his incompetence and slothfulness. When humourists sharpen their pen at his expense. When the public, in search of someone to blame for their economic woes, begins its dreary chorus that there are too many bureaucrats . . . This is of no concern to the senior public servant, for he has unshakable faith in his role, in his star, his indispensable nature. His pride flows from his longevity, fidelity, legendary loyalty to the government in power, whichever one it happens to be. Strength and reason are on his side, not to speak of patience, and he will need the latter quality to ignore the repartee and insults, the *bons mots* and adverse opinions of the commentators. He who knows does not speak. He will triumph in the end. He will endure. He is Loyalty, Duty and Honour.

Not to mention that, by hanging onto his position, come what may, he can go on cashing his cheque every two weeks, with a clear conscience and a peaceful heart.

∞ ∞ ∞

The mandarin takes pleasure in knowing that his remuneration is slightly higher than that of certain important, highly reputed persons he has always admired and envied and emulated. Professionals, scientists, even men of letters. Secretly, he is astonished that not only has society permitted such an anomaly to occur, but has done nothing to correct it. The mandarin thanks his lucky star and keeps his mouth shut, just as he seals his lips when the young check-out girl gives him back change from a twenty, instead of from the five-dollar bill he handed her.

∞ ∞ ∞

Carefully observe that which the senior bureaucrat has given you, be it an object, a piece of advice or a service. You will notice its contours strangely resemble those of a boomerang.

∞ ∞ ∞

For the senior bureaucrat, to possess a state secret is a considerable honour. It affords him great pleasure. In his universe, one must be of a certain rank and position to know something that must not be divulged. With contempt and condescension, he gazes upon those whose lives are simple and peaceful and who know nothing worth concealing.

These budgetary constraints are so bothersome. They force the mandarin into all sorts of administrative pyrotechnics to reach his goals. But he does reach them, even if it means his life is a just that much more difficult.

Take this trip to London that he is planning. His assistant needed three whole days — he had to contact the British High Commission and even purchase the *London Times* — before unearthing some official event compatible with his ministry's mandate, in this case the testing of an ultramodern radar system in a high-tech plant in the suburbs of the British capital. Of course, it also happened to coincide with another event, this one more personal in nature, the true but hidden goal of the mandarin's trip and which, for reasons of discretion, one is better off not mentioning . . .

How can you even think such a thing? The mandarin has no intention of acting furtively, for he has nothing to hide. He will travel to London for a valid State mission, something to do with radar. And while he is there, he will use the opportunity — at his own expense, of course — to attend the other assignation, the one you know about, which you will keep under your hat . . . There is no shameful behaviour in any of this. Besides, three of his fellow mandarins visited London last year, and he certainly has a right to it this time around . . . But that's not what's at issue. What counts is the official reason for the trip, which any journalist on the Hill can see, and you know what they're like! Forever scratching and burrowing every which way, even taking aim at the bureaucrats with that insatiable appetite of theirs, instead of turning their attention to politicians and ministers. They even ask questions about the trips senior public servants occasionally take, even those which have been perfectly, painstakingly justified by the mandarinate, whose integrity is legendary and brooks no expressions of doubt . . .

∞ ∞ ∞

The high-ranking bureaucrats form a very selective club who have taken the vow of facelessness. But unlike members of certain religious communities, they have taken no vows of chastity or poverty. They may savour the pleasures of love and relative wealth, out of the gaze of indiscreet observers, undetected by all.

∞ ∞ ∞

Senior public servants are content with samples, tendencies, averages, projections, approximations. Except for their pay cheques, of course, which must always be perfectly accurate or, in any case, must contain no errors to their detriment.

∞ ∞ ∞

Democracy, says the senior bureaucrat, is for the masses, like beer, hot dogs, liberated women and affordable housing. My tastes run more to good whiskey, steak, my secretary and my renovated apartment near Parliament.

∞ ∞ ∞

Concealed within the enormous brass statue which is the upper-echelon bureaucracy, gazing undetected through the eyes, nostrils and mouth of the impassive and all-powerful goddess, the mandarins, like the high priests of Antiquity, lend their hoarse, monotonous voices to the oracles received with such avid trepidation by the enslaved and trembling tribe of petty bureaucrats. They have carried with them sweet nectars and choice morsels to seduce the divinity and win over its favour. Gently, the practical-minded senior public servants accept these gifts, for they know that the tin goddess cannot know the meaning of hunger or thirst.

∞ ∞ ∞

For the high-ranking mandarin, true wealth, supreme luxury, is to have attained that level where one no longer has any need of others.

∞ ∞ ∞

It is a source of pride for the senior bureaucrat to know his name is inscribed on some scrap of paper buried deep in the government archives. One gets the sort of immortality one deserves.

∞ ∞ ∞

In order to work for the betterment of his province, and contribute to the streamlining and healthy administration of his ministry, a certain member of the mandarinate sacrifices himself and unwillingly accepts the dirty job of firing — or at least identifying for the executioner — his colleagues, underlings, even friends, one by one, cold-heartedly, like animals ripe for the slaughter. And once the messy business is over, and the cries of the victims have fallen silent and their blood washed away, he will tiptoe out from his hiding-place behind the filing cabinet to ask for the promotion negotiated for and promised at the outset (of course there was no contract, but one's word suffices, and simply a hint or a meaningful smile is legal tender when one is among honourable men). Now, what about that job as Assistant Deputy Minister in a ministry of his choice?

∞ ∞ ∞

The comfortable sofas that line the offices of senior public servants can actually be used for sitting on.

∞ ∞ ∞

Affirmative action is a fine invention bestowed upon us by politicians and mandarins. Its purpose is to extend to women, the handicapped, native people, persons said to be of colour and soon (perhaps) to senior citizens — the list keeps growing — the special favours, questionable promotions and privileges that once were the exclusive domain of insiders, colleagues, friends, girlfriends, family, people from the same school or discipline, etc. A fortunate occurrence, all in all. For it ensures the democratization of injustice, which means a greater number of citizens may enjoy it. It is the victory of small justices over Justice — but only temporarily, you understand . . . The subjection of the general good to the particular need, the perfect example of the ends justifying the means. At last injustice is harnessed and made available to all, recycled, dressed up in its Sunday best and made to serve fairness. The Devil serving tea to the Lord above.

∞ ∞ ∞

Just as the pleasure of garlic discourages the enjoyment of love, so the pleasure of being a senior bureaucrat destroys the possibility of enjoying other pleasures which he once held dear. Common vintages spoil the palate for fine wines. One must choose. And choosing is a process of elimination.

∞ ∞ ∞

The cocaine addict soon can no longer do without his drug, and finds himself at the mercy of his suppliers; and so a lower bureaucrat quickly develops the bureaucratic habit. The longer the habit lasts, the more difficult it is to change careers, as he grows older and more specialized, and slowly loses the skills and knowledge to do anything else. And then there are practical considerations: one's pension plan and the bother of moving.

The senior bureaucrat stands aside and watches the situation develop. As time goes by, as the underling stumbles and bogs downs, as it becomes more difficult for him to back out, the senior public servant makes his presence felt. Little by little, quietly, smoothly, in calculated doses, he makes his weight felt, subjects the subordinate to low tasks, shameful compromises, humiliating downgradings. In the end, he has acquired a docile and submissive slave, whose financial needs, social stability and lack of alternative solutions force the poor underling to remain in his job, come what may. Ultimately, like the cocaine addict, he may even agree to refined and abstract forms of fraud, theft and prostitution.

∞ ∞ ∞

In a literal sense, we could not say that a senior bureaucrat, having witnessed an automobile accident, would be more concerned with the victims' wallets than with the victims themselves. But figuratively, that is exactly what occurs. Because, you see, in his world, the victims do not bleed, they do not moan for help, they have not been deprived of a limb. And so it is that a certain senior public servant will insist that *he* was the first to claim the large, handsome office — the one with the huge windows — vacated by the death or shelving of one of his colleagues.

∞ ∞ ∞

If a senior bureaucrat tells you he despises wealth and is happy simply "serving," as he likes to say in the intransitive mode, satisfied with the modest remuneration the government is willing to give him, do not think you are dealing with a man of virtue, abnegation or altruism. The truth is that wealth is out of his reach, since it requires from those who deserve and obtain it higher qualities than the ones found in the world of the mandarinate. In real life, there is an entirely different and infinitely stricter code of merit, based on the attributes and demands of the world, which have almost nothing to do with the intrigues, influences and whole range of small virtues and peccadilloes that constitute the bureaucracy's daily bread.

One exception to this rule: when the senior bureaucrat leaves his job and joins a private corporation, he acquires a temporary usefulness, as he has become a kind of high-class stool pigeon ready to sing on the Public Service, and teach others how to get the most out of it, setting himself up as go-between. This form of treason has become so popular and lucrative lately that senior bureaucrats who have remained temporarily faithful have had to establish new rules to stem the tide. But if the "faithful" ever had the opportunity to cross over to the private sector, they would soon find a way to sidestep the very regulations they themselves created, and whose loopholes they know so intimately.

∞ ∞ ∞

A certain senior bureaucrat built himself an enviable reputation for having brought a mediocre and lifeless project to term. He enjoys a far better rating than his colleague who failed to implement an extraordinary, even brilliant project, which was, however, difficult to accomplish.

"The moral of the story," according to a well-known senior public servant, "is not to waste your time on major undertakings. Do as I do: settle for small triumphs. It's more profitable."

∞ ∞ ∞

When a senior public servant does you a favour, he expects that, sooner or later, you will return it. In fact, he is merely lending you the favour. Doing himself a deferred favour.

∞ ∞ ∞

The top bureaucrat hesitates: the offer is tempting. It's a dream opportunity to join a dynamic team that the mandarin of mandarins is about to set up. It will have unlimited funds, discretionary powers over the rest of the federal Public Service, it will one day make recommendations likely to change the power relations between the Legislative and the Executive, it will provide privileged status for its members and an enviable opportunity for fame . . . The top bureaucrat still hesitates at length before accepting the offer. All will depend on the primordial question, the ultimate condition: will I get my own parking space?

∞ ∞ ∞

Is a senior public servant giving you effusive thanks? It is because he hopes to secure other benefits from you. If you yield, and provide them for him again, he will thank you once more with the same effusion. Which puts you in the position of having to continue doing him favours. Now you are a prisoner in a vicious circle. If, on the other hand, at the outset you refuse to do him the slightest favour, you remain free. You gain nothing, of course, but you lose nothing either. Except for the senior public servant's thanks.

∞ ∞ ∞

The main difference between a top bureaucrat and a petty clerk is in the pay cheque. The rest is debatable.

∞ ∞ ∞

The charismatic mandarin capitalizes on the prestige he has acquired in his underlings' eyes; the admiration they express; the honour they feel at being able to serve him; their eagerness to foresee his least desire; their ability to understand unsaid his more or less legitimate aspirations; their spontaneous support whatever the circumstances; the quick, clean execution of confidential errands; their loyalty, good will, discretion . . . Do you think these are abstract dividends? You are mistaken. For sooner or later, through slow, mysterious but inevitable means, these abstractions always convert into cold, hard cash.

∞ ∞ ∞

Senior bureaucrats are highly sensitive to the honour their rank provides them: to have more office space than they really need. On the other hand, they are insensitive to the malaise of visitors who are struck by the obvious disproportion between the grandeur of the room and the pettiness of its occupant.

∞ ∞ ∞

If you closely observe the actions of the mandarinate attending a wine and cheese reception, you will notice they frequently prefer the wine and the cheese to the company of the other guests.

∞ ∞ ∞

Because of what he knows and what he does, the senior public servant experiences concern, suffering, even unhappiness. On the other hand, what he does not know and does not do are for him inexhaustible sources of peace, joy and quietude.

∞ ∞ ∞

Senior bureaucrats are like those one-armed bandits in American gaming houses. Probability is on their side, and they merrily pocket substantial profits simply by allowing themselves to be solicited by naive and hopeful players, who stuff them full of coins.

∞ ∞ ∞

If victory is not guaranteed, the senior bureaucrat will withhold judgement and stay on the sidelines. But if it is within reach, he will move quickly to the winners' side and join their celebration, the better to make off with his share of the booty.

∞ ∞ ∞

A certain senior public servant who has always displayed scrupulous honesty in small things will never miss a chance for dishonesty when the opportunity for an enormous, unexpected, one-time profit presents itself. A slumbering reflex will suddenly spring to life and a well-oiled mechanism is set in motion. Just as a bear will efficiently kill the first time its anger is aroused.

∞ ∞ ∞

Like maple syrup from the Laurentians, fruit jams from the Okanagan or smoked salmon from the Pacific, injustice for the senior bureaucrat is a luxury product designed for moderate, even sparing use. Once the crumbs of elementary justice have been distributed as they must be to the underlings — even as he advertises the virtues of merit — the senior public servant will closet himself in his office, at a restaurant or in even his own home. There, alone or in the company of a few trusted friends, sheltered from the excessive demands of equity, common sense, honour, morality and, most of all, from those thousands of soul-killing rules and regulations, he will determine and carry out the secret strategies that will painlessly procure him this result, that advantage, or this gain. The way poorer parents treat themselves to a good bottle of wine and take the steak out of the refrigerator once the children have been stuffed with noodles and are safely in their beds, asleep.

12
In the Public Eye

⟨decorative ornament⟩

The senior bureaucrat never lunches with a colleague who, from all indications, cannot be of any use in his advancement in the foreseeable future. Except for days of inclement weather, which keep him close to the office and force him to settle for whatever company he can find. Or during the slack periods of vacation time, when people of quality are few and far between. Or he may chance upon some lustreless colleague just as he was about to sit down to a solitary lunch, his intended guest for that noon having had to cancel at the last minute.

In the same way, he will not lunch with a colleague from whom he has already solicited a favour, when there is little chance he will be useful a second time.

But he will gladly lunch with a man who, he knows, will attempt to solicit a favour from him and, to increase his chances of success, will insist on paying the bill.

∞ ∞ ∞

The mandarin will open his black umbrella only when it rains. Otherwise, he uses it as a sort of fetish to embellish the movements of his person, display proof of his foresight and elegance, soothe his anxieties, keep his countenance, and occupy his hand and wrist. Just as, every evening at Thebes, the Greeks count off their worry beads.

∞ ∞ ∞

When a vulgar individual acts aggressively toward him in the street, ignoring the lofty rank of his victim, using insulting words or threatening gestures, the senior public servant stays calm. He does not respond to the aggressor and elegantly steps aside. A witness to this scene may well wonder: was the action self-containment and strategy or, instead, cowardice and the instinct for flight?

∞ ∞ ∞

The charismatic mandarin presides. With his grave voice displaying his depth, weight and self-assurance, he reminds his colleagues of the necessity to maintain the enviable reputation of honesty and objectivity enjoyed by top bureaucrats, then reviews with them the major ethical principles upon which the Public Service is founded. As, at the same time, he reaches into his pocket and feels for the smooth shiny nail he furtively picked up in the street over lunch hour.

∞ ∞ ∞

Especially at noontime, the mandarin avoids going down into the street where he may meet all manner of ordinary people, talking and laughing loudly, eating spicy, inexpensive things from fast food outlets, cutting past him on the sidewalk without a glance of recognition or a display of regard for him. Or, worse, recognizing him, greeting and even trying to speak with him, obliging him to respond, if only for a moment or two, to keep from projecting that despicable image of a cold, inaccessible, haughty character. Commending themselves to him, reminding him of this or that service performed, asking for a meeting, a promise, a favour . . .

The mandarin prefers restaurants a bit off the beaten track, but not too distant, to which he can walk if skies are clear or, if it is snowing, drive, taking his car from the heated underground garage. Though he won't turn up his nose at the downtown restaurants, as long as they are well soundproofed, if the staff is discreet and recognizes the establishment's privileged clientele, if the light is sufficiently filtered, if the finest *digestifs* are served;

in other words, if the atmosphere is propitious to exchanges of wit, whispered confidences and smiles, unofficial dealings, unwitnessed promises, expressions of trust among colleagues, verbal agreements, secrets that must be kept. But best of all are the restaurants at the Parliament buildings. Not only are the meals subsidized, one meets only elite diners there. The greatest of the great public servants, those other bureaucrats who are powerful but of uncertain rank floating in this ill-defined zone where political power meets the mandarinate, hordes of petty MPs without influence — that is, without a budget — wooing the senior public servants and even ministers of government.

Then, other times, the senior bureaucrat will turn his back on these myriad temptations and stay to work in his office, and have a sandwich brought up by his secretary-waitress.

∞ ∞ ∞

His pace is quick and decisive. Wherever he goes, even if it is for a walk, the senior bureaucrat moves at top speed. If you accompany him along the sidewalk, he is always one step ahead of you and, rather than slow down, he will turn around to converse — or should we say continue his monologue? If you grow tired of always lagging behind and seeming slow or tardy compared to him, and you drop your natural pace and speed up to reach his level, he will take that as a sign that he's shaken you from your lethargy. Or, perhaps, that you intend to compete with him. Because, you see, competition in all its forms is his specialty. He will then speed up his own pace, wiping out the effort you have made, so that in the end you have not gained any ground at all. This faster rhythm soon wears you out, and you fall back to your usual pace, losing sight of your mandarin friend in the crowd ahead as he goes his merry way, unperturbed, gesticulating, explaining his point of view.

∞ ∞ ∞

Just to have his statue in the park, the senior public servant would gladly put up with all its pigeons.

∞ ∞ ∞

As long as he stays in his office or presides in a conference room, the senior bureaucrat soars with the grace of an eagle. He moves masterfully, powerful and magnificent, in an artificial universe whose privileges, rules and obligations he is well versed in. But once he goes down to street level, he becomes a colourless little sparrow. Like everyone else, he must endure the tyranny of traffic lights, the pressure of the crowd, the line-up at the bank. What mortification! None of these people have any inkling that there is a prince among them. Surely they would open their eyes wide were they to discover it . . . That truck driver there, for example . . .

"What did you say your name is? No, I don't know you. If you don't mind, the line begins back there. Everybody waits their turn here."

∞ ∞ ∞

When a senior public servant dies suddenly at his desk, most people will remember only the ambulance parked in the fire lane that day, lights flashing. Then even that memory will fade.

∞ ∞ ∞

To meet a senior bureaucrat in the street can be a traumatizing experience. Your eyes tell you beyond a doubt that you're on level ground, while all the mechanisms of your body are functioning as though you were descending a steep grade.

∞ ∞ ∞

If you are dining in one of our capital's restaurants, take our advice and hide the book you are reading in your briefcase. This will spare you your superior's ill will and the disapproval of the mandarinate. Unless, of course, your book is in Braille.

∞ ∞ ∞

Instinctively, the senior bureaucrat knows he must never be seen lunching alone. This could point to some social flaw in him, some tribal dissonance, or idiosyncracy of dubious taste, a worrisome independence of mind, an imperceptible straying from organizational ethics. This is the kind of behaviour that can suddenly set off the complex and mysterious mechanisms of his eventual downfall.

∞ ∞ ∞

If a senior bureaucrat absent-mindedly peruses a newspaper as he dines, that is acceptable. If he pages through a file folder, well, all right. But if he reads a book, especially a thick one with a hard cover, he has committed an unpardonable offence. There are, after all, limits to bureaucratic savoir-faire that must be respected.

13
Friendship

∾⧟∾

For the senior bureaucrat, friendship is to be consumed, like a Vichyssoise or a ripe Stilton, but only at the opportune time, after it has reached a sufficiently advanced point that the greatest possible benefit may be derived from it.

∞ ∞ ∞

Friendship among senior bureaucrats is a sad, difficult and passionless affair. Like love between a man and woman who are physically ugly, and have settled for one another after a thousand vain attempts to interest more attractive partners.

∞ ∞ ∞

Do not trust the senior public servant who speaks to you of friendship. For he knows that sooner or later, in some way he himself may not yet imagine, you will be useful to him.

∞ ∞ ∞

The senior bureaucrat does his best to retain the friendship of a colleague who has fallen into disfavour. Especially if he has not had the time or opportunity to benefit from this friendship. He continues to invite him to lunch, but in far-flung, obscure restaurants, or in discreet dining rooms not usually frequented by their colleagues.

The senior public servant will not hesitate to resort to friend-ship, if he must, to reach his goal.

∞ ∞ ∞

If he is to be fashionable and in tune with the times, the senior bureaucrat must update his friends, as he would his wardrobe.

∞ ∞ ∞

It's to the mandarin's advantage to express pity over the downward curve of a colleague's career. This provides him with an occasion to give a public display of his compassion and the shock he feels, which will solidify his reputation for loyalty and fidelity toward his friends. All this, without putting him under any obligation to provide any help whatsoever.

∞ ∞ ∞

Most often, members of the mandarinate speak of their friends in the past tense.

∞ ∞ ∞

From the very first day he takes the job, the senior bureaucrat begins to exert an influence upon you. A sort of humid pressure, a viscuous attraction, a suction that may become deglutition. An effect of agglomeration and agglutination by which he seeks to assimilate you to his interests, associate you with his strategies, force you into interminable acquiescences, reduce you to a silent partner. He will transform the relations you have with him into a kind of sleazy camaraderie, and your nascent friendship into a perpetual prison.

∞ ∞ ∞

When a senior public servant denigrates himself — for ex-ample, by admitting that his memory is not what it used to be, or volunteering the opinion that his last presentation to the management committee was rather weak — he is secretly hoping that, out of friendship, you will contradict him. That you will fight to persuade him the opposite is true, and that in the end you will triumph and succeed in defending — with all necessary proof — a different opinion than his, which happens to be flattering to him. He would be most disappointed were you not better than he is at this game.

Whatever you do, do not be intimidated by the strength of his arguments against himself. They will be vigorous and hard-hitting. Your job is to find even more vigorous and hard-hitting ones. He wants nothing more than for you to beat him, and he will be happier the more convincing, violent, even brutal you are. That is when he feels the most pleasure in being defeated.

∞ ∞ ∞

The senior bureaucrat almost always saves his friendship for those more powerful than he. Since it is necessary, even unavoidable to love someone, sooner or later in this life, runs his reasoning, it might as well be a person who, if the occasion presented itself, could serve his interests and advance his career.

∞ ∞ ∞

Friendship between top-level bureaucrats is often of short duration, because they soon demolish the wall of appearance that each erects between himself and his counterpart. Each has little appreciation for what he discovers behind this wall. And so their contacts become less frequent, then disappear. Yet each mandarin is so satisfied with what he perceives in himself that he cannot understand the disgust his colleague feels toward him. Just as one's own odour is sweet, and those of others offensive. It's best to wash one's hands of it all, so they think, keep one's distance and write off this lost friendship.

∞ ∞ ∞

Astonishing, the way a certain senior bureaucrat can use the means at his disposal to resolve a difficulty to your advantage by sidestepping a rule, or astutely eliminating one of your competitors, or encouraging you with such overwhelming enthusiasm that you are embarrassed, but still flattered . . . Beware. After you have gone, he will do the same for the next person. Perhaps at your expense.

∞ ∞ ∞

If a senior bureaucrat has recovered rapidly from the misfortunes of his best friend, it is often because he contributed secretly to his downfall, in the hope of procuring some personal benefit. In the same way, when he can do nothing to stop his best friend's success, he makes an about-turn and rejoices, subtly suggesting that he somehow contributed to it, in hopes of procuring some personal benefit.

∞ ∞ ∞

The mandarin stops gracing you with his friendship the very moment he realizes he won't be needing you in the foreseeable future.

∞ ∞ ∞

When a senior bureaucrat looks at you with a penetrating gaze, remember the warnings you have heard about AIDS.

∞ ∞ ∞

When a senior public servant gives you a friendly piece of advice, rest assured that he first thought of how he could take advantage of it. He serves his own plate first. If there are any leftovers for you, that's nice, but not essential. Besides, "giving a friendly piece of advice" is a metaphor, since the senior public servant never gives anything. If he parts with something, it is always for strategic purposes.

∞ ∞ ∞

The mandarin's pain at the death of a friend and colleague is sincere and profound. Will he ever find anyone with such a high opinion of him as his late colleague had?

∞ ∞ ∞

The tears a top-ranking bureaucrat displays at a colleague's funeral are not for the dear departed. They are aimed at the living he will meet at this grand occasion who, seeing his pain, will revise upward their opinion of him.

∞ ∞ ∞

The senior bureaucrat has many friends who don't like him very much, and many enemies who don't dislike him very much either. These two classes of people are often the same.

All of which isn't very inspirational, of course. But it's still better than having many enemies who dislike him strongly, and many friends who don't like him at all.

∞ ∞ ∞

Forced to choose between keeping a friend and keeping a secret, the senior bureaucrat will spare the former and sacrifice the latter. Because, like virginity, secrets have a negative value. They can be used but a single time; they have no value until they have been taken advantage of. The senior public servant will opt for immediate consumption, keeping friendship in abeyance, with its wealth of potential services and future benefits . . .

∞ ∞ ∞

When with his one-eyed friend, the senior bureaucrat always sits on the side with the sightless eye.

∞ ∞ ∞

If, despite all our exhortations, you decide to let yourself go and develop a deep friendship with a member of the mandarinate, be our guest! Just remember to keep your parachute on at all times.

∞ ∞ ∞

The senior public servant gladly shares his misfortunes with his friends, but he's much less generous when it comes to his successes.

∞ ∞ ∞

Promotion has a disastrous effect on the visual acuity of top bureaucrats. The more promotions they receive, the more difficulty they have recognizing former friends in the street.

∞ ∞ ∞

The senior bureaucrat turns to friendship only in cases of personal danger. As an atheist will pray to God when his plane is going down.

∞ ∞ ∞

Friendship with a senior bureaucrat can only be the result of a misunderstanding.

∞ ∞ ∞

The senior public servant has so many friends he can afford to sacrifice one from time to time, without it being noticeable. Just as he might take a fine bottle from his well stocked cellar for a special occasion. Which he will replace at the first opportunity.

∞ ∞ ∞

Often friendship will flourish between two powerful public servants who have fallen into disfavour and darkness. Attraction and solidarity are not the keys; rather, obscurity is, and the lack of heat. Their friendship has the hue of a mushroom grown in a gardener's dark cellar.

∞ ∞ ∞

A senior bureaucrat who may not be picky about his friends will display the greatest circumspection when it comes to the choice of enemies. The latter, you see, are generally more durable. He tallies up their age, state of health, rank, influence, supporters, talent, etc., determining factors in the struggle and its outcome. Besides, these enemies are perfectly reversible. By pressing one button instead of the other, he can transform them into friends if he ever concludes that, when all is said and done, conciliation makes for better business than confrontation.

∞ ∞ ∞

Avoid making a top-ranking bureaucrat a friend and comrade. He will sacrifice you at the first opportunity, in line with the austere tradition of the greatest good for the greatest number. And for his own greatest good, of course, since — as coincidence would have it — the interests of the group are almost always synonymous with his own.

∞ ∞ ∞

The senior bureaucrat puts much faith in the healing, idealizing effect of time. Take this colleague he offended in the past. One whom he had no desire nor occasion to meet since then, with whom he is officially on bad terms. The passage of time, he knows, will slowly darn the tear in the fabric of their relations; it will render invisible the needle's mending and even obscure the circumstances that led to the break. In the end, it will create the illusion of unworn, virgin cloth. Everything goes back to normal. The colleague becomes a sort of provisional friend from whom the senior public servant can once again derive some benefit — by creating a new conflict with him if necessary — if ever a valid occasion presents itself.

∞ ∞ ∞

A senior public servant's friendship is like a well-formed nut we open, laboriously, carefully, only to discover there is no meat inside.

∞ ∞ ∞

The mandarin is a sociable creature. He never misses the opportunity to make new friends. A fortunate disposition, considering the great number he goes through.

∞ ∞ ∞

The senior bureaucrat serenely accepts that, with disconcerting regularity, today's friends will become tomorrow's enemies.

∞ ∞ ∞

Friendship serves as a way of determining merit among senior public servants. Sex plays the same role when the two genders of public servant mingle. At times, appointments to high-paying positions give off a between-the-sheets smell. This is as it should be. It proves — as if it needed proving — that on the scale of bureaucratic merit, coitus and friendship have about the same weight.

∞ ∞ ∞

Among the mandarinate, friendship is not a sentiment. It is a decision.

∞ ∞ ∞

A colleague is drowning. The senior bureaucrat offers a helping hand, then draws it back, hesitates, wonders if he might not be saving the life of an eventual rival. This hesitation can go on for hours.

∞ ∞ ∞

Friendship among senior bureaucrats often hibernates. For months at a time, sometimes years, it slumbers, neither expressing itself nor deteriorating in any appreciable way. Then, as the mild spring air awakens a bear, it shakes off its lethargy when a pressing need or perfect opportunity comes along. The senior public servant takes telephone in hand and calls his old friend to invite him to lunch and cash in, at long last, on the profits of this long-term investment.

∞ ∞ ∞

Friendship among top-ranking bureaucrats lacks those binding and crystallizing agents. It is poor in precipitants. It has no ardour, substance or fire. It easily dissolves in frivolity, teasing, comic effects. A little like camaraderie among chortling, mischievous eighty-year-olds merrily awaiting death in a nursing home, pulling at each other's dressing gowns after lights-out, hiding one of their fellow's slippers or comparing urine samples in the daylight . . . Where have you gone, David and Jonathan?

14
Status

⚓

Mandarins are like those megalithic statues on Easter Island, in the Pacific. In vain, we seek to understand by what miraculous intercession these heavy, inert, monstrous sculptures could have landed there, what primitive, mysterious genius could have fashioned them, what powerful, unseen lever could have erected them and set them there for all eternity.

∞ ∞ ∞

Top-ranking bureaucrats never lend their names to mountains, rivers, polar islands. They are too high, they flow too far, they set out such terrifying obstacles. On the other hand, senior public servants do escape anonymity by having their names engraved in white letters on a black plastic rectangle, which they proudly display on their desks.

∞ ∞ ∞

That which is important in the eyes of a senior public servant certainly cannot be as important as all that.

∞ ∞ ∞

For senior bureaucrats, punctuality does not mean showing up at the appointed time. It refers to the appropriate time, given the quality and rank of the colleagues involved. Those who arrive before or at the appointed time are lowest on the hierarchical totem pole. Those who come after the appointed time are weighty personages; the last ones to enter the room are the cream of the crop. As for those individuals who show up after the cream, they are simply late.

∞ ∞ ∞

The senior bureaucrat comes slowly into the conference room, cuts left while looking right, manoeuvres skillfully, moves around the circular formation of his colleagues without joining them, slips past them, applies a fake to an underling who tries to accost him, extends his neck to look over the heads of the assembled multitude, answers a question with a smile and an evasive nod of his head, moves in closer, then stops at the strategic point, neither too near nor too far, perfectly even with the Minister being interviewed as the cameras whir. He will move his lips slightly as if talking, open his mouth as if listening attentively to an invisible speaker, then stare into the camera's eye with deliberate nonchalance, smiling discreetly, slowly turning to show his most favourable profile after which, casually but with perfect naturalness, he will leave the camera's field of vision, and disappear.

That evening, the senior public servant will appear on national television.

∞ ∞ ∞

In his mind, at least, the senior bureaucrat has already begun his departure from this world. He is floating away from this lowly sphere where it gets muddy when it rains, where cars break down, sometimes, between the office and the airport, where the refrigerator stops working late on Friday evenings, where he needs a hammer to knock in that nail in the closet which twice tore his suit. Nothing upsets him more than this complex universe of innumerable and varied objects with which he must co-exist, and get used to, which ceaselessly demand his attention, which are dirty, broken, too big or lost, which insist that he pick them up, feel them, measure them, rub them, screw them in, strike them, paint them or simply throw them away. As much as possible, the senior public servant avoids or ignores or forgets them, better to devote himself to his own private, chosen universe that he has created, and which alone interests him. A refined, abstract world full of such issues as national policies, strategic meetings, logistical considerations, brainstorming sessions, fall-back positions, overall perspectives, exploratory studies, unofficial negotiations, interprovincial coalitions, incompatible software, matrix structures, critical pathways, progressive integrations, programmed scheduling, renewal of provisional or obsolete agreements. This is no grab-bag of gibberish, as the jealous, uninitiated enemy maintains. On the contrary, it represents a superior universe in which, alas, there is no room for a sputtering lawn-mower engine, nor for the damage done to the kitchen ceiling by a leak from the shower upstairs.

It took the senior public servant some time to understand this, but now he knows. The proof: he has chosen to rent a luxury apartment rather than own a house in the country. Minimized his contact with sweat, dust and all those things made of wood, metal and plastic that stand between him and cerebral activity, his constant ascent toward superior abstraction. Toward an aerial, etherized existence, freed as much as possible from material, constraining, tyrannical objects. Toward an atmosphere of rarefied air and razor-sharp, luminous, intense concepts that take him and transport him far away, which are better than a rocket ship of dreams, requiring all his time and energy. Concepts that forego any long-term, serious relation with power-saw handlers, summer-cottage builders, camping fanatics, handymen with dirt under their nails and brains forever encumbered by a thousand scraps of practical knowledge.

∞ ∞ ∞

With his hand on the flusher, perplexed, hesitant, the senior bureaucrat is absorbed in thought, unable to decide if that really is his reflection he spies at the bottom of the bowl.

∞ ∞ ∞

The senior bureaucrat uses profanity, since it is the fashion of the day, but he does so with moderation, staying within the limits of good taste. Not that he is naturally inclined to use such language, nor does his type of work demand that the heavens, its inhabitants and the world's more familiar processes be called upon, named, disturbed, shaken and battered. Not at all. But there is a code, non-verbal and non-written — always the most tyrannical kind — that all senior public servants must respect if they wish to remain at the cutting edge of fashion and organizational savoir-faire . . . But that's not quite it. Or rather, that's not all there is to his language filled with handsome, vigorous swear words scattered with such aplomb throughout the conversation. If the senior public servant does not blaspheme at all, he will be labelled as a hypercultivated individual, intellectual, careful, still bogged down in Judaeo-Christian tradition, incapable of bold thrusts, moderate excess, creative innovation or virile anger. A single profane oath delivers him from this menacing host of demons who threaten to dull his star, cast him into the common grave of insignificance, transform him into a characterless being, colourless, devoid of energy and life itself.

Yet the senior bureaucrat must be careful not to sin on the side of the other excess. An overly rich variety of profanity, an overly frequent appeal to its magic, a manner that betrays too great a naturalness and sincerity, coupled with a lower-class accent, a certain inability to distinguish situations in which swear words are not indicated — this is a dangerous combination for the senior bureaucrat, who must then hasten to defend himself against the reverse image. The image of a mediocre individual whose natural character comes galloping back as soon as he lets down his guard, who blasphemes not out of strategy or aesthetic concern, or to confound the petty pencil-pushers and shock the right-thinkers, but simply because swearing is part of his being, his primary culture, his past social milieu, which up until then he forcibly repressed and cleverly concealed. The image of a vulgar individual who stumbled into his present rank by some accident or act of mistaken identity, all astray in a superior society that he has deceived as to his qualities as a human being. The image of a bureaucrat with no subtlety or finesse, who violates the elementary rules of Christianity, its conservative spirit based on tradition, balance, respect for social and even verbal conventions . . .

"Yes," the senior public servant would agree, "blasphemy is an indispensable but difficult art."

∞ ∞ ∞

Let us pray that, in the next world, the bureaucrats we encounter there will not be those we know on Earth. Where they are fatally the same, year after year. Where they succeed each other, one after the other, exchanging titles and positions, but remaining unmovable members of the same closed society . . . the way a sitting man shifts from buttock to buttock, but still remains seated.

∞ ∞ ∞

Any idea that may spring from a senior bureaucrat's mind contains its own limitations, if only because of the mind that gave birth to it. The flowering will produce dandelions, not orchids. One does not escape from what one is, or from what one must be.

∞ ∞ ∞

When choosing his career, the bureaucrat must resign himself to this sad fact, even if he reaches the upper echelons: no one will ever ask him for his autograph.

∞ ∞ ∞

Some men settle for less and consider themselves lucky to be above all suspicion, free and unchastened. Not the senior public servant. It's not good enough for him not to get caught, and for his honour to be secure. He demands more than that. He wants your understanding, your trust, your friendship, your intimacy . . . And even that is not sufficient. He clamours for your consideration and respect, even your admiration, and not the kind spontaneously displayed by his obsequious underlings

— because in the end it becomes automatic, monotonous, with no real meaning. He wants the admiration of quality people, the kind he himself holds in high esteem, of which you are a member, at least temporarily. You see, serving the nation is no easy task. A man like him must make difficult, often painful, decisions. Actions somewhat less than honourable are involved, low blows, at times, though he squirms to admit it . . . Which is why, in return, he demands the compensations of the mind, a little social pick-me-up, some generous, concrete, palpable encouragement . . . What can you do, someone has to take care of the dirty work. Just be glad that someone isn't you!

∞ ∞ ∞

Key bureaucrat. Important public servant. Wonderful oxymorons. Inadvertent word-play.

∞ ∞ ∞

There are circumstances in life that lead people to join a scuba-diving club, or a genealogical society, or an association of friends of the horse. Other circumstances lead other people to blend into the diffuse and unclear society of the mandarinate, though no one can say what random succession of events, often obscure, could have produced such a result. Yet the mandarinate has somehow acquired a sacred right of belonging, an innate sense of appartenance, a member's card of the mind. The way other members of other clubs may clothe themselves in the discreet pride of those who appreciate the mysteries of the deep, or the symmetrical tree of ancestors or the grace of galloping horses.

∞ ∞ ∞

The difference between a bureaucrat and a senior bureaucrat resides in the adjective "senior." Note that it could just as well qualify one as the other. A fine example of the multi-use, interchangeable character of senior public servants.

∞ ∞ ∞

A member of the mandarinate behind the wheel of a BMW . . . A bizarre anomaly: the machine is superior to the man.

∞ ∞ ∞

Their career has not led to wealth, nor esteem nor glory; senior bureaucrats console themselves by turning to two favourite strategies, often used simultaneously. The first is to discreetly suggest that, moved by noble, ascetic feelings, they purposely sacrificed fame and wealth, better to devote themselves to the welfare of the State and its citizenry. The second is to do whatever necessary — in other words, everything and anything — to obtain the highest possible salary and garner at least some local success. Which consists of fame in the eyes of their underlings, in the enclosed, straitened, miniaturized universe that is the federal bureaucracy.

∞ ∞ ∞

The senior bureaucrat truly and sincerely believes he has achieved greatness, and is secretly offended if others do not recognize this quality in him.

∞ ∞ ∞

In the social hierarchy, the senior bureaucrat is the only important character who has never done anything great or important to earn his standing.

∞ ∞ ∞

The senior public servant does not fear winter in our northern climes. At times he does not even don his overcoat. He travels from one underground installation to the next, from one heated garage to the other, in a car as warm as toast. On weekends, he does his shopping in luxury boutiques burrowed underground, in a friendly crisscross of tunnels, basements and galleries, all brilliantly decorated and brightly lit.

When he is weary of the depths, or when duty calls, he takes the elevator to the heights of one of our capital's skyscrapers, be it his apartment or his office, according to the hour of the day; both overlook Parliament . . . But he doesn't ride to the very top. The next-to-last floor is preferable if one wants to avoid the noise and inconvenience of elevator motors, and the various ventilation, exhaust and heating systems. There, in his generous living space, he dwells in silence and warmth.

No, the senior public servant does not fear winter in our northern climes.

∞ ∞ ∞

A great thinker has said: man reaches his greatest heights when he is on his knees. The senior bureaucrat would revise that to read, When he is sitting down.

∞ ∞ ∞

Among the human race, senior bureaucrats are the only ones who do not bury their dead. They let them dry in the open air, on specially designed shelves. They are allowed to leave these shelves and move freely through government offices and the streets of the capital, on the condition that they not disturb the tribe of living bureaucrats busy rewriting documents or raising objections in meeting rooms. Needless to say, this contempt for traditional sepultures has some unpleasant side effects. For example, as well as occupying choice office space in the city centre, these defunct public servants create uncertainty and confusion wherever they go. Out of some mischievous spirit, no doubt, they infiltrate and mix in with their living colleagues so well that no one knows whether they are dealing with a dead bureaucrat or a living one. They seem to take a perverse pleasure in the ambiguity and uncertainty as to their status. Sometimes it takes months, even years, before one can be entirely sure of their state.

We should applaud the generous attitude of these living mandarins, who have chosen to put off as long as possible their colleagues' definitive passage into the great beyond, where their tragic, eternal destiny awaits them. But, then again, their sojourn on this earth is of such insignificant duration compared to eternity, and since no one can do the slightest thing about it, the best solution would be to bury them quickly, and put an end to all this confusion.

∞ ∞ ∞

When you enter a room where a reception for senior bureaucrats is being held, and notice the thick cloud of smoke gathered around the ceiling, do not be mistaken. The smoke does not come from cigarettes. It issues from the combined action of incense-burners that sycophantic public servants bear in their hands as they go about introducing themselves to one another, or seeking to please a colleague or curry favour from a superior.

∞ ∞ ∞

The mandarin likes to put time between himself and others, between inactivity and his next initiative. Just as the writer leaves empty space between his paragraphs, the musician silence between the notes, the painter great washes of pure colour above the landscape. Immediate speech and action seem improper, unacceptable to him. His thought must be allowed time to come to maturity, events must be distilled, his person needs time to ripen and develop like a perfume, to take on volume, to come to fruition. He resists those who would disturb his dignity, and violate the imaginary space he has drawn around him. He counters plans that call for immediate action. If necessary, he will change a deadline, put off or miss a meeting, forget to return a telephone call, let a unique occasion go by. Too bad! Too bad for the others, who should have recognized him for what he is, a person to be reckoned with, to be consulted, a VIP, a true personality . . . Once this complex message has gotten through, been not only understood but accepted, only then will the mandarin agree to move, with all due deliberation . . .

∞ ∞ ∞

The senior public servant often displays an elevated opinion of himself, but rarely an elevation of the spirit.

The bureaucrat knew how to reach the top levels of the bureaucracy. He accelerated quickly, attained a proper cruising speed, entered into his chosen orbit. He knew one must soar above the crowds, over the heads of the common people. After that, everything is easy. Like riding a bicycle: once you learn, you never forget.

Soon, the new senior bureaucrat will acquire a weighty reputation. His colleagues will be used to seeing him soaring through the heights, and no one will imagine that one day he might have to return to earth, like the rest of us bipeds. And they are right. For he has taken on the aura of a minor god. He flits from privilege to privilege, promotion to promotion. He is the subject of every conversation, the man of the hour. He is solicited for all the highest positions and boards of directors, his name will make the project, give it that touch of prestige. Then soon, he will crumble under the weight of these honours.

∞ ∞ ∞

Do you know why a senior bureaucrat never achieves fame? Because fame is born, takes root, and endures only when the means taken to reach it are perfectly clear, above all suspicion and doubt. Otherwise, it quickly sours, turns into notoriety, then disappears.

∞ ∞ ∞

It is essential for a senior bureaucrat that others have a high opinion of him. You see, he cannot quite convince himself that he has any value, or is worthy of esteem. He knows all the little details about his thoughts and actions that no one else knows, and they keep him from perceiving himself as a man worthy of consideration, a man of principle, of importance. Obviously, if others knew what he knows, they would draw the same conclusion.

∞ ∞ ∞

I know of a certain senior public servant who savours the sovereign's easy gesture when, from his throne, he summons the loyal subject and bestows awards upon him, or inflicts punishment, as the case may be. Without anyone inquiring why, without having to offer the slightest justification, his royal blood sufficient to raise him naturally above the crowd and spare him those petty explanations about his being or actions. The senior public servant aspires to royalty. Even a minor fiefdom would suffice.

∞ ∞ ∞

Given his untouchable status, the senior bureaucrat can accumulate rare and remarkable faults and vices, to which he would have never acceded if fate had condemned him to remain in ordinary mediocrity. Instead of reaching high-class mediocrity.

∞ ∞ ∞

The mandarin does not possess the boldness of action, the ambition, presumption, footing, reach and span of his model and master the politician — though he does strive to emulate him. If he wins, he wins less, of course. On the other hand, if he loses, his losses are smaller, too. To each his proper measure. Such is the order of things.

∞ ∞ ∞

The senior public servant avoids attending meetings wherein participants are few or low in the hierarchy, no matter the importance of the subject at hand. He is aware that his presence benefits the government — a marginal issue to him — but does not see how he himself will derive anything from the proceedings — the primary issue. A man whose time and inner resources are as precious as his should spend his time in more useful pursuits. Upon this noble thought, he excuses himself from the meeting room.

Once safely in the hallway, another thought nags at him. Here was a meeting loaded with bureaucrats who, besides being of inferior level, were incapable of appreciating the quality of his comments and the impeccably greased wheels of his logical mind. As well, his true colleagues — other senior public servants who might spread word of his competence — did not bother to show up, or even send a replacement. Obviously, he walked right into a trap. I'd better be more careful in the future, he promises himself. Which means choosing meetings more likely to display his talents and contribute to his advancement.

∞ ∞ ∞

When he is late to a meeting, the top-ranking bureaucrat will never excuse himself. Instead, he expects that, out of deference, the chairman of the session will interrupt the flow of the meeting and sum up what has been said up until that point, while the others wait . . . The chairman, who is also a senior public servant, is glad to do that, either because the latecomer is in a position to be useful in a certain pet undertaking of his, or because he will do the same for him at a later occasion. A simple exchange of niceties among civilized people. While the others wait . . .

∞ ∞ ∞

Forced by life's circumstances to concern itself solely with petty detail, the mind begins to accept its fate, feel comfortable in its yoke and excel in its miniature world. But on the way to this acceptance, it gives up those greater things for which it has slowly become unsuited. With the passage of time, these grand quests become dry, abstract, "philosophical" issues. Example: the minds of the mandarinate.

∞ ∞ ∞

Senior bureaucrats are to society what utensils are to a well-laden table. Nothing more.

∞ ∞ ∞

When a senior bureaucrat's reputation has been seriously stained once, no cure is possible; recuperation and remission are out of the question. It hardly matters if he is to blame, or whether the culprit was the force of circumstances beyond his control. All that matters is the primal stain in his colleagues' perception. An automatic, inexorable, fatal mechanism comes into play and begins devouring him alive, the way a frog slowly disappears into the jaws of a snake. He may clamour and protest and declaim his innocence, beg forgiveness — all is in vain. His colleagues become deaf and blind. They know only that life is like that, and every so often fate designates one of their number as flesh for the sacrifice, the way the farmer chooses the unlucky turkey among the flock for his Christmas dinner.

The swift downfall of our unfortunate bureaucrat begins. He ceases all forward progress, he stumbles, he falls backward. He is marginalized, isolated, immobilized, ostracized. He may manage to hang onto the bureaucratic machine and, with a little luck, succeed in his quest to be forgotten, to survive and live out his career, long enough to finish raising his younger children and pay off the summer cottage. But the days of soaring are over forever. He will never regain his original innocence.

∞ ∞ ∞

Bonaparte said that a throne is but a plank of wood covered with velvet. Not the senior bureaucrat's chair: it is constructed from chrome-plated metal, rare wood, synthetic fibres and cloth, flexible plastics, rigid cardboard, metal parts of different shapes, springs of variable tension, wheels of complicated design, axles, pivots, levers to set the inclination and the tension, washers and sheets of foam, glue, nuts, bolts, toggles, etc. Which proves that the status of the bureaucrat is infinitely more complex than that of a mere emperor.

∞ ∞ ∞

The senior public servant is in constant war against the condition into which he has been forced by his occupation, and does his best, despite the odds, to look like the rest of humanity.

A career in the higher echelons of the Public Service is almost always a compromise, an alternative plan, a fall-back position, even a last-chance solution.

∞ ∞ ∞

The grandeur of the mandarin comes from his rank. A shame it couldn't come from a more natural, personal source.

∞ ∞ ∞

A senior bureaucrat is a man standing up in the sitting position.

∞ ∞ ∞

The respect we give the mandarin flows more from his rank than from his qualities. This is an insult and he knows it, but one he gladly accepts, as long as we continue to respect him.

∞ ∞ ∞

What's so irritating about the senior bureaucrat is that, with absolute sincerity and conviction, and without the slightest trace of scheming or strategy, mediocrity assumes an appearance of competence, a pretence of excellence.

∞ ∞ ∞

We say, *A top bureaucrat*. We never say, *A great bureaucrat*. As if we sensed instinctively the comic contradiction the latter term expresses.

∞ ∞ ∞

A freshly appointed mandarin entering his new organization is a ball of fire at first. He blitzes the staff, and they show him respect and subservience. From both sides of the fence, there is observation, spying, evaluation, gauging, suspicion. Extreme caution is to be observed, until both sides have established the other party's intentions, character, determination, courage, way of working. Then little by little, familiarity takes over. The staff measures the length of the new boss's chain, they get used to the whiteness of his teeth, his furious leaps forward, his loud but meaningless barking. Everyone soon discovers his unkept promises, unexecuted threats, catalogue of clever expressions, the little routine of this representative of upper management. Then, finally, the cat falls asleep on top of the dog.

15
Culture

Whether at the corner tavern or in the office of a senior bureaucrat, avoid quoting Milton or reciting Shakespeare.

∞ ∞ ∞

After attending the theatre or a concert, the mandarinate speak of their enchantment, and how moved they were by the cultural experience they had. They applaud with authority, profusely, as do their spouses, especially when it comes time for the curtain calls. It's a shame they can't do the same at the cathedral, when the grand religious organs fall silent after a final crashing chord, or in their favourite French restaurant, as the Sauternes and the Béarnaise sauce clamour for their gastric juices.

∞ ∞ ∞

In his free time, the senior public servant enjoys looking into philosophy, poetry, aesthetics, the way others grow cucumbers or do macramé. He has the same respect and esteem for philosophers, poets and artists as he has for gardeners and textile artisans. In other words, an acute interest mixed with a kind of sympathetic contempt. "They work in 'soft sectors,'" he says.

∞ ∞ ∞

Sisyphus was probably a senior bureaucrat. In any case, the resemblance in their occupations is striking.

∞ ∞ ∞

The senior bureaucrat is a serious appreciator of art. And since paintings are given him free of charge by the government, he asks for a dozen of them to be brought into his office, so he can choose the ones he prefers, exercising his highly developed aesthetic knowledge, his insatiable need for what is beautiful and his innate penchant for art.

"Let's see . . . no, not that one, there's too much green in it and green really isn't in fashion this year . . . Not that one either, because of the pink, which isn't quite the right colour to go with my secretary's new fuchsia skirt . . . That painting is too big, there wouldn't be enough room between it and the ceiling . . . and if you bring it down, it's simply too close to the rug . . . There's too much black in this one, it gives the room a funereal atmosphere . . . Take that one away, too. Its light oak frame clashes with the rosewood bookshelves . . . As for this other one, it might not be very handsome" — notice the critical faculties at work — "but it does have one advantage: it's a perfect fit for the empty space behind the door; I won't even need to move the curtains. Put it aside for now and let's see the next one . . . Ah, that's it! That's my favourite, the one with our Lord and his apostles seated around a large oval table. Doesn't it just remind you of the Senior Management Committee meeting? And what do you know, the apostle who is breaking bread with Jesus Christ looks exactly like me . . . That's incredible! Yes, that's the painting I want. It will be the centrepiece of my office."

∞ ∞ ∞

The person we wish to be spoils the person we are, says the moralist . . . Except for senior bureaucrats, of course. In their case, they are better off taking the risk.

∞ ∞ ∞

A certain senior public servant of our acquaintance, upon returning from vacation in Spain, brought a libel suit against the Prado, after recognizing himself in a canvas by Bosch.

∞ ∞ ∞

The cultural knowledge of the upper-echelon bureaucrat is a form of lubricant that allows him to be invited and accepted in the social setting and environment of his choice. Once he has succeeded and settled into a comfortable position, he can easily do without any lubricant. Penetrating is the hard part. After that, everything goes by itself.

∞ ∞ ∞

The senior bureaucrat thanks his lucky stars that modern chemistry has made such progress. For now it is easy, with today's detergent formulas, to totally bleach away the blood stains that once caused Lady Macbeth such worry.

∞ ∞ ∞

For the modern reader, Hell as imagined by Dante is over-stated, naive and not very frightening. What may have inspired terror in the peasantry of the fourteenth century leaves today's population cold, or even makes them smile. How can we believe in the rain of fire, the marshes of the Styx, the lakes of boiling blood, where bodies rather than souls are tortured and suffer?

If Dante could return to this life and revise his Comedy, there's no doubt he would situate his Hell in the federal senior bureaucracy. Instead of conceiving of divine vengeance as punishment against the body, he would certainly employ the genius of his imagination to depict a hideous Hell founded on mental torture and aberration. Therein, spirits would be tormented by routine, by documents forever rewritten, security problems and promotions. Minds would be preoccupied by strategies, ruse and petty vengeance. True thought would be laughed at, atrophied or non-existent. Lame bureaucratic reasoning would stumble badly but win the race. Ideas would be compromised by arrogance, starchy self-importance, blind certainty and an unhealthy sense of authority.

∞ ∞ ∞

Vaguely, very vaguely, the old bureaucrat remembers azure water, a child's cry, the smell of fresh cut hay, the heat of a stone in the sun. But he banishes these evil thoughts and turns back to his scribbled lines, the only universe that counts . . . the only true reality.

∞ ∞ ∞

When the princess in the fairy tale kisses the frog, it changes into a prince charming . . . But what if things had turned out differently? What if it had turned into a high priest of the mandarinate? Or if the princess had kissed a senior public servant? Or if the frog had kissed a high-ranking bureaucrat? Or if . . .

∞ ∞ ∞

Just as Monsieur Jourdain was astonished to discover he spoke in prose, the senior bureaucrat is all amazed to discover that management is simply the exercise of common sense. But in both cases, a teacher is necessary.

∞ ∞ ∞

Eunuchs do not sing. Neither do senior bureaucrats.

∞ ∞ ∞

Never offer to lend a book or a record to a senior bureaucrat. He will think you are mocking him, and his bitterness will be your reward.

∞ ∞ ∞

The *hoi polloi* generally believe there's nothing wrong with cheating the taxman, that, in fact, it's to be commended and all means at one's disposal should be used, good or bad, to avoid paying taxes. Likewise, senior bureaucrats believe it is their right to be amused and entertained by the minds and intelligence of others, authors and artists especially, in their books, at the theatre and through music, but in such a way that the bureaucrats, the public Treasury or even the public at large will not have to spend a penny, or as little as possible. They believe it is normal — after all, isn't this part of their legendary charm? — that those who wish to live off intellect and art should be poorly remunerated, as they have always been, penniless, concerned only with fame.

And speaking of fame, senior public servants enjoy nothing more than lifting a glass of champagne in places where authors and artists meet, as a way of sharing a little of their glory, so that this fine gold dust may fall upon them, too, upon their suits of British wool, with the perfect pinstripes . . . As long as someone else is springing for the champagne. The government, for instance.

∞ ∞ ∞

The philosopher Rivarol must have been thinking of the mandarinate when he wrote, "It is a terrible advantage to have done nothing, but one must not abuse it."

∞ ∞ ∞

There are exceptional cases when a senior bureaucrat acts so perfectly like a gentleman that nothing is noticeable.

∞ ∞ ∞

The senior public servant derives continual pleasure from rereading his documents, and discovers in his most arid texts strokes of genius that either he did not intend, or which had escaped him up until then.

∞ ∞ ∞

Have you ever noticed that members of the mandarinate never write their memoirs at their careers' end? Of course not! Why would they want to bring their careers to other people's attention? Why would they want to remember themselves? Besides, what could they possibly write that anyone would want to read?

16
Personality

Senior bureaucrats are like those little figures cut out of several thicknesses of paper, then unfolded to the enchanted eyes of children, who laugh at their appearance, so completely alike, attached one to the next through a chain of solidarity. Except that, instead of holding hands, senior bureaucrats hold onto each other's tails.

∞ ∞ ∞

His finger — index finger, to be exact — stops suddenly, wavers, then begins moving, aimlessly so it would seem, around his nostril. Then the finger climbs toward the ear, and on the way meets the security of the beard hairs, where it lingers a moment, before slipping casually behind the ear lobe and heading for the nape of the neck. Then it disappears into the hair, accompanied this time by the other fingers. It emerges again, hidden in the anonymity of the hand which, in a quick, involuntary movement, is joined by the other hand, as the ten fingers come together and cross and stretch . . .

It's too late. We saw you, Mr. Deputy Minister. Next time, close your door. From the hall we saw you jab your index finger deep into your nostril. Its movement was insistent, gyratory, graceless, as it impatiently reamed out some blocked chamber.

∞ ∞ ∞

The senior bureaucrat: this giant, malodorous hot-house flower that did not respect the destiny written in its seed. That did not draw nourishment from its root, nor keep the promise of its bud.

∞ ∞ ∞

Among the mandarinate, dignity is often a defensive position the body assumes when the mind is unable to face the music.

∞ ∞ ∞

A senior bureaucrat is like an onion. One by one, you remove the skins in which it is wrapped, behind which something seems to be concealed. Only to discover, in the end, after you've removed the final layer, that there is simply nothing at the centre. Not even a pit. Behind this succession of concentric appearances, you expect to find marrow, a kernel, a seed, some kind of vegetable heart. But you are mistaken; your hopes are in vain. Appearances do not hide its substance; they *are* its substance.

∞ ∞ ∞

We wear these masks, say the senior public servants, because we have no faces.

∞ ∞ ∞

The animal shows its gratitude by eating from the hand of its benefactor. The senior bureaucrat shows his gratitude by eating the hand of his benefactor.

∞ ∞ ∞

Members of the mandarinate often take on the appearance of a pregnant woman in her last month. Protruding stomach, waddling walk, careful movements, solidly seated, digestion delicate but demanding, ample clothing in sober hues. Unfortunately, in their case, the miracle and grandeur of motherhood are not present; discomfort is not rewarded. There is no birth, not even a miscarriage. What's worse, this state lasts much longer than nine months.

∞ ∞ ∞

A certain weakness in a lower-level bureaucrat may be unforgivable. In a senior public servant, that weakness becomes a charming part of his personality. Admiringly, the underlings will repeat the hurtful words he growled in his gruff voice.

∞ ∞ ∞

Thinking is the primary cause of a senior bureaucrat's wear and tear.

∞ ∞ ∞

Whatever happens, there will always be a senior public servant to say he expected it. Prophet after the fact.

∞ ∞ ∞

The senior bureaucrat who systematically refuses to agree with anyone often cannot brook other people's opinions. Even his stupidity is consistent.

∞ ∞ ∞

Today, the senior public servant has ten dollars to spend. Will he buy a Mozart record or eat *steak tartare*? He hesitates. He struggles valiantly. But the stomach, always the stronger competitor, wins out over the mind.

∞ ∞ ∞

We know that many geniuses had the reputation for being absent-minded. Their minds were so intensely and entirely absorbed by a great concept, project or monumental plan that they would forget to carry out the petty routines that daily life demands. Their brains were overloaded, overexcited, filled to the brim, so that they could no longer cope with everyday demands. Among the mandarin class, on the other hand, absent-mindedness betrays the boredom of a mind with nothing to save it from spinning its proverbial wheels. Its thought, objective and motivation produce little heat, and often go no further than the desire for a cup of coffee, the hope of a postponed meeting, the impatient wait for the weekend. Its reflexes atrophy and slumber, since they are seldom used.

∞ ∞ ∞

Senior bureaucrats believe they have a God-given right to waste other people's time.

∞ ∞ ∞

The mandarin is always right. When he is obviously wrong, refer to the previous sentence.

∞ ∞ ∞

The senior bureaucrat loves applying a rule no one else knows, discussing a book no one else has read, quoting a person no one else has met, talking about a radio program no one else has heard, describing a city no one else has journeyed to . . . It's so much easier to win when there is no competition.

∞ ∞ ∞

The thoughts of a senior public servant often have bad breath.

∞ ∞ ∞

The mandarin is a mutant form of life. In the footsteps (so to speak) of the swimming coelacanth, the crawling mammal, the four-legged hominid and *Homo erectus*, along comes the Sitting Man: the senior public servant.

The mandarin class is like gases in chemistry. The lightest ones tend to rise higher and more quickly.

∞ ∞ ∞

The senior bureaucrat is fond of his navy-blue vest with the white pinstripes. He would wear it if his colleagues wore theirs. But they have turned their backs on the style this year, except for a few who valiantly hold out, trying in vain to bring it back into fashion. Against his own personal preference, our public servant will leave his vest in his closet, out of fear of being associated — in his mind and in others' — with the minority, were he to wear it.

But fashion is so changeable! Just in case it turns again, he will buy the full three-piece suit when he chooses his next suit, better to scramble back with the majority public opinion, if need be.

∞ ∞ ∞

It's always a pleasant surprise when you step into a senior bureaucrat's office. The smell is not at all the one you were afraid of.

∞ ∞ ∞

Jesus' thirteenth disciple was a senior public servant. But seeing that Judas was already at the table, he took his leave.

∞ ∞ ∞

Every morning, the model mandarin settles into his routine and wallows in his habit with a kind of frenzy.

∞ ∞ ∞

The nervous, tormented behaviour of some senior bureaucrats speaks of the constant war within them. On one side is the appeal of integrity, which urges them toward openness, honesty and sincerity. On the other side, the siren call of strategy, which pulls them toward intrigue, concealment and furtiveness. This struggle creates a zone of turbulence that knows no respite, like the point where the Saint Lawrence and the Saguenay come together, as these two great rivers mingle their current and their colour.

∞ ∞ ∞

A senior public servant never dies for a great cause, a lofty principle, or an extraordinary undertaking. He simply dies.

∞ ∞ ∞

The mandarin is irresistibly attracted by the smell and taste of water. Call it a case of affinity.

∞ ∞ ∞

The senior bureaucrat wears his best cologne on his days off.

∞ ∞ ∞

"For a moment," a senior bureaucrat tells it, "I thought I had gone beyond the harsh limits that my own DNA, my genetic inheritance, placed upon me. The awakening was hard. Reality is ungenerous. I will never know the drunken joy of flight the great migrating flocks feel."

∞ ∞ ∞

Often, deafness brings speech. You don't see my point? Example: when a senior public servant begins to speak, it means he hasn't been listening to what you were saying. At least, he didn't hear it . . . Though, sometimes, he starts talking when, by all evidence, he is still listening to you, and therefore, must have heard you . . . Let's revise our paradox this way: hearing brings speech as well . . . But none of that really matters. The important thing is the result: you have been consigned to silence.

Warning to members of the mandarinate: continuous wearing of masks obliterates the face.

∞ ∞ ∞

Age reveals the true quality of the human being. When the senior public servant's initial supply of charm dries up — his hair, his looks, intelligence, ambition, loyalty — at the time of his retirement, there remains a distilled, primordial substance, a dry grey matter which is something like the very foundation of his being, a kind of nakedness which he cannot escape. Makeup and screens fall away. Here, DNA becomes visible.

∞ ∞ ∞

When we say of a senior bureaucrat that he is adding weight and volume, we are inevitably speaking of his body.

∞ ∞ ∞

Behold the old bureaucrat in retirement. Speaking in loud tones, gesticulating, hoping to seduce or at least cajole, puffing up his ego like the breast of a pigeon — no one listens to him now. Deprived of his function, he is nothing, and that is not easy to get used to. Astonishment: his money is no longer legal tender, his gruff voice frightens no one, his rules are outdated. His temporary, artificial universe upon which he staked everything falls to bits. He is the perfect prototype of the throw-away human being.

∞ ∞ ∞

Senior bureaucrats feed essentially off Little Red Riding Hoods. But for variety's sake, sometimes they will devour one of the three little pigs, or some poor lost lamb.

∞ ∞ ∞

The mandarin displays remarkable affinities with the monkey, donkey, cow, pig, dog, horse and a host of other animals.

The proof? Many of his activities have him monkeying around, making an ass out of himself, cowing people, lining up at the trough, etc.

∞ ∞ ∞

The senior public servant hopes for sunshine, if only to wear his sunglasses, which he would wear all the time, if not for that unfortunate convention according to which one doesn't wear them unless the sun is out. His insatiable appetite for masks, the desire to observe unnoticed, the need to crouch under cover of darkness, to take shelter behind obstacles, to mask his roving eye that is forever giving him away, to hide his vulnerability like some shameful organ, to project this impassive image so dear to all highly placed bureaucrats, so essential in the quest for promotion. The senior public servant, that supreme master of concealment, dreams of a cloudless country undarkened by night, in which he could wear opaque lenses forever.

∞ ∞ ∞

For the mandarin, that which is honourable is also idealistic, and therefore philosophical. In other words, impractical and not very profitable.

∞ ∞ ∞

The senior bureaucrat sticks close to the hero as the latter makes his way through the applauding crowd, so that some of the fame may spill onto him. In the minds of the uninformed, so the bureaucrat hopes, the hero's face will be associated with his, since they have been seen together. Perhaps this will help provide a more brilliant, lasting career . . . Let us understand and forgive him, for he is of those who are eager for fame, though unfortunately, she does not return the favour. One does what one can . . .

∞ ∞ ∞

A senior bureaucrat we know could never understand why the house plants he is forever buying refuse to survive in his apartment. They shrivel and die after a few months of pained, stunted existence. Yet the sun pours in and there is a proper amount of water and fertilizer in the rich, pest-free earth . . . Could there be some truth to this common pseudo-scientific opinion according to which plants can detect and understand the thoughts and feelings of human beings who share the space with them?

∞ ∞ ∞

The senior public servant has stopped searching. He has triumphed over doubt. He has found what he was looking for. He is happy.

∞ ∞ ∞

We know of a certain mandarin who emanates dignity, to such a point that it stinks. The way some people smell of perspiration.

∞ ∞ ∞

The caricature does not look like the bureaucrat; the bureaucrat looks like his caricature.

∞ ∞ ∞

The senior bureaucrat is an essentially diurnal creature. Like the crocus, he closes at dusk. In the evening and at night, he lives a diminished, effaced, larval life; he almost seems to fade in with the rest of us common mortals. As in a science-fiction film, it is difficult to detect the evil aliens invading the planet Earth, who hide inside robots that perfectly mimic the human body, or in real human bodies they have stolen after having expelled the rightful owners.

∞ ∞ ∞

If the primates had decided to walk on their hands instead of their feet, human beings' sitting position would have been compromised forever. This would have slowed humanity's evolution for thousands of centuries, ruling out the invention of the oval seat and the bureaucrat's armchair.

∞ ∞ ∞

Senior public servants suffer from the acute dichotomy between thought and action. If they declaim a principle or rule or opinion in your presence, do not think that action will follow suit. That which makes them speak is not necessarily, or even at all, that which makes them act. In phrenology, the phenomenon would certainly be explained by the fact that the thought centres of senior public servants are to be found on the left side of the brain, whereas the action centres lie on the other side.

∞ ∞ ∞

Some days, the mandarin is consumed with energy. He functions furiously, running from meeting to meeting. To save time, maybe even to keep his balance, he bends his head in the direction he is going when he negotiates a right-angle turn at the end of a hallway.

∞ ∞ ∞

A certain senior bureaucrat believed he had become paraplegic. Actually, he had both feet in the same shoe.

∞ ∞ ∞

Like all humans, senior bureaucrats descended from the apes. Some of the former seem to be ascending again.

∞ ∞ ∞

In the mind of the mandarin, love and fornication are congruent.

Great minds use few words to say much. The senior bureau-crat uses many words to say little.

∞ ∞ ∞

Between a lying compliment and a justified expression of blame, the mandarin will always choose to listen to the former.

∞ ∞ ∞

Some senior bureaucrats are akin to poodles. They have no use and frighten no one, but they are excellently turned out, have a style of their own, and make pleasant company.

∞ ∞ ∞

The senior public servant enjoys idling in that murky zone between hesitation and immobility.

∞ ∞ ∞

If they are unsure about something, most people will say nothing. When a mandarin is unsure, he will speak a little faster and a little longer than usual.

∞ ∞ ∞

For peak production, the senior bureaucrat needs a certain minimum level of darkness.

∞ ∞ ∞

Senior public servants amaze us. Not because of their large number of vices and faults, but because of the rarity of their vir-tues and qualities.

∞ ∞ ∞

The dignity of an ordinary public servant is almost visible, almost palpable. It is like the sacerdotal vestment the priest puts on before a religious ceremony. It is like the slick and shiny oil the athlete rubs on his body before the race. It is something like the sad, gentle mask of madness, just before a lunatic grimace or a meaningless word betrays it.

The more intelligent members of the senior bureaucracy employ dignity with more taste and moderation.

∞ ∞ ∞

Take these murky speculations, dubious theories and nebulous theses about the anti-hero in the modern era . . . Why, the senior bureaucrat has always been there, the most perfect model one could hope for . . . Besides, he is alive, and real. In palaeontology, he corresponds to the discovery of the coelacanth, that once swam and continues to swim in the waters off the Comoro Islands, even as scientists were vainly searching for it among prehistory's fossil collection.

∞ ∞ ∞

Behind his apparent simplicity, the mandarin hides a true duplicity.

∞ ∞ ∞

The senior bureaucrat scurries from the room, offended, seething, insulted that they have chosen a younger competitor over him to fill a coveted position. Officially, in loud tones, he declaims his contempt for those who humiliated him this way, and his intent to seek vengeance as soon as . . . What? The chosen candidate has turned down the job? The senior public servant returns to the room, excuses himself for his temporary absence — you understand, there's an intestinal flu going around . . . He sits down, having forgotten the affront, clinging to hope once again.

∞ ∞ ∞

When it comes to his honour, the mandarin is always ready to accommodate.

∞ ∞ ∞

Among the mandarinate, strength of personality is made of four ingredients: high self-confidence, coupled with a great capacity for bold action, both of which are served by mediocre, or average at best, judgement and knowledge. The formula has been thoroughly proven through testing, and has produced some triumphs of stupidity.

∞ ∞ ∞

A senior public servant can continue to look at you, whether he is coming or going. The only problem: you don't know which of the two faces is the mask.

∞ ∞ ∞

It has now been scientifically proven beyond a doubt that the telepathic flow emanating like a vapour from the DNA of a senior bureaucrat has a direct influence on the person in his office creating, in the latter, in a relatively short lapse of time, a kind of hypnotic, soporific slowing and numbing, whose most obvious effect is to rapidly augment the tension of the muscles of the lower mandible, causing the mouth to open and remain open. In other words, a yawn.

∞ ∞ ∞

"You must be careful with senior public servants," said the cannibal to his son. "They are like mushrooms. They all look alike. But some of them are edible, while others are violently poisonous."

∞ ∞ ∞

The senior bureaucrat has no regrets about being what he is. For remorse to take hold, there would have to be a point of ref-

erence, a comparison. For example, he would have to be someone whom he is no more, or cease being what he was. But the
senior public servant never was anything other than what he is
today. Except for normal changes brought about by the passing
of time, nothing suggests that he will be any different tomorrow
from what he is today, and what he always was. Everything indicates that the senior public servant will be what he already is,
and what he has been. He will die, equal to himself, the perfection of horizontality.

∞ ∞ ∞

Let us observe the workings of the mandarin's mind in his
native habitat. We may be inclined to speculate that, had the
challenge been different at the start, he might have been capable
of great things. But the occasion was never there; he could not
abstract himself from his milieu and rise above it. It came to possess him completely and define his being with its own limits.

∞ ∞ ∞

No, take my word for it, the senior bureaucrat is not attempt-
ing to hide. This is his natural behaviour. Curious, isn't it?

∞ ∞ ∞

The retired senior public servant sits on a bench in a covered
shopping plaza, in the middle of the luxury boutiques and hur-
ried crowds, elderly, upright, impassive, white-haired. Near
him, a woman is seated whom he does not know, elderly, upright, impassive, white-haired. The former hooker who passed
herself off as a market vendor, better to attract the customers.
Both of them with banked fires, serene, eyes distant and vague,
stiff in their authentic but recent dignity. Without passion or past,
without memories to cherish. Empty eyes staring into their brief
futures.

∞ ∞ ∞

Never turn down the occasional appointment with a mandarin. It is a way of reminding yourself how sweet your own company is, after passing time with him.

∞ ∞ ∞

Appearances obsess the senior bureaucrat to such a point that he literally has no time left to be what he really is. But let's suppose he had the time and occasion to be himself. The reality of it would be so desolate that he'd be better off being something else. Which brings us back to our point of departure. The more we think about it, the better off everything would be if nothing changed at all in the senior public servant's life. Let appearances triumph over being . . .

∞ ∞ ∞

What good would it do if senior public servants had wings? They would simply go nowhere faster.

∞ ∞ ∞

We are struck with sadness when gazing upon a member of the mandarinate in a good mood. The way we might feel faced with the good humour of an optimistic invalid.

∞ ∞ ∞

When he is among his colleagues, the senior bureaucrat will scratch at his buttocks. When he thinks he is alone, he will scratch himself a little lower, with application and insistence. Seen from the front, the hem of his pant leg would jump and dance above the tip of his well-polished shoe.

∞ ∞ ∞

To delve into the being of one senior bureaucrat removes all desire to get to know others.

∞ ∞ ∞

The mandarin who laughs loudest usually laughs hollowest.

∞ ∞ ∞

There are times when, rising from his armchair, a senior public servant will forget to conceal his tail.

∞ ∞ ∞

The senior bureaucrat hates random chance, for it resists him, disobeys him with impunity. How can it be brought back into the fold? How can it be tamed, then vanquished? He dreams of domesticating random chance, as others dream of harnessing lightning.

∞ ∞ ∞

By some curious, reverse alchemy, that which seemed clear and luminous at the outset becomes obscure and shadowy after passing through the crucible of the mandarin's mind. Instead of growing lighter, more refined, instead of taking wing, ideas grow heavy, thicken, contract. The process is inverted: gold is transformed into lead.

∞ ∞ ∞

Evidence disperses objections. Except for those put forward by senior bureaucrats.

∞ ∞ ∞

The chatterbox talks more than he listens. The senior public servant talks more than he thinks.

∞ ∞ ∞

To embark upon discussion with a member of the mandarinate, to attempt to inform or persuade him is like pouring good wine into a bottle already full to the brim with tap water.

We sometimes suspect that the senior bureaucrat is suffering from a sprained brain. That would be impossible, of course. But the analogy helps us better understand the functioning and workings of his mind.

∞ ∞ ∞

The senior bureaucrat's sadness flows from this: he pays too much attention to himself. Instead, he would be better keeping his sight fixed on something more exciting, more inspirational, more sunny.

∞ ∞ ∞

Is a senior bureaucrat polite with you? It is a merely transitory stage brought on by the initial, imaginary distance that separates you from him. Quickly, as he moves closer to you, the mirage will dissipate and courtesy will give way to familiarity. Should that occur, fasten your seat belt.

∞ ∞ ∞

The mandarin will gladly answer you, but on one condition: that you not attempt to link the answer directly and flat-footedly to the question you asked him.

∞ ∞ ∞

Generally, a senior bureaucrat will remain standing only if he cannot sit down.

∞ ∞ ∞

When a member of the mandarinate makes a promise to you, he is, in fact, providing you with valuable information. You can then go about organizing your life around the premise that he will not keep his word. Or, at least, not the way you thought he would, or at the time you were counting on.

Even when he is physically standing, the senior public servant is sitting down mentally.

∞ ∞ ∞

When a senior bureaucrat makes an endless speech, his exasperated partner in conversation may perceive what his nose would interpret as a nauseating smell.

∞ ∞ ∞

My lengthy observations of the mandarinate have procured me infinite pleasure. Because of this, I will never be a successful bureaucrat, for the latter's pleasure consists in knowing he is being observed. Apparently, one penchant excludes the other. But I would be the last to complain; you see, in both cases, the satisfaction each feels is its own proper and sufficient reward.

∞ ∞ ∞

The senior bureaucrat would be a man of greatness, if only he had done something great. That is the only factor that stands between him and greatness. All the other components are there.

∞ ∞ ∞

Among the mandarinate, dignity and certainty are diseases, pathological states, as are leprosy or herpes. They will not kill you, of course, but they make life miserable, and are a constant menace to others.

∞ ∞ ∞

At times, senior public servants will let themselves go, in an attempt to relax when the atmosphere becomes too tense. They become mischievous and teasing, like children all over the world. Except that they give the unmistakeable impression of being children born of elderly parents.

∞ ∞ ∞

The mandarin has nothing over the minimum. Everything in him is functional.

∞ ∞ ∞

Among senior bureaucrats, it is often difficult to distinguish between dignity and a stiff neck.

∞ ∞ ∞

Senior public servants can be separated into two main categories: those who seek promotions and those who get them.

∞ ∞ ∞

Members of bureaucracy are the opposite of solar batteries. Sunlight paralyzes them, whereas their energy and efficiency increase in the darkness.

∞ ∞ ∞

The senior bureaucrat has understood the primary virtue, which is to resist, maintain oneself and endure. Instinctively, he will choose the strategic fall-back position, the pow-wow, the negotiated settlement, the compromise, the conciliation session, the temporary setback, the smokescreen, the tactic, the delaying of deadlines, etc. He has no sense of those actions in the code of military honour which are translated by expressions such as coming face to face, sounding the call, leading the charge, firing when ready, hand-to-hand combat, tightening the ranks, fighting till dawn, winning a bloody battle, spilling one's blood, giving one's utmost to the best of one's ability, death before dishonour, losing the battle but preserving one's honour, dying with one's boots on, etc.

∞ ∞ ∞

The senior public servant is like that spare part left over when you've finished repairing a machine and it's working well.

Frequenting the mandarinate can't help but remind you of New Brunswick's famous Magnetic Hill. Even though you feel you're climbing, you're really descending.

∞ ∞ ∞

When you seem to hear the roaring of a senior bureaucrat, do not be alarmed. There must be a lion in the area. But if you hear the telltale *hee-haw*, then you know there's trouble.

∞ ∞ ∞

A quick glance is all the senior bureaucrat needs to determine whether a certain colleague is worth greeting. If he isn't, he will walk past him on the sidewalk without a nod, pretending to be looking at his watch, ignoring the colleague who is pleasantly greeting him. But when the situation is reversed and someone else does not return his greeting, our public servant wishes he had never issued the greeting in the first place. He is so mortified that he will refuse to greet the next colleague he meets, in revenge and out of compensation, suspecting him anyway of having no intention of greeting him. Yet, if his expectations are confounded and the colleague does greet him, but at the very last moment, leaving him no time to return the greeting, he will regret not having greeted him earlier and fear that, next time, the colleague will not greet him, out of spite and vengeance, while he, on the other hand, may have already greeted him, and it will be too late to draw back his hand and avoid the humiliation of having greeted someone without having been greeted in return.

The life of a senior public servant is so stressful . . .

17
Morals

The senior bureaucrat will never reach the point of being above all suspicion. But he consoles himself knowing that, at least, he is untouchable.

∞ ∞ ∞

The mandarin hesitates between craft and honesty. He suffers the temptation of nobility of spirit and asceticism. But craft wins out, for it is his first love, his path of predilection.

∞ ∞ ∞

Like the Catholic church through the ages, like tavern bouncers and females in a moose herd, the senior public servant invariably chooses the winner's side. He lets the weak and the vanquished fend for themselves, no matter how appealing they are, no matter how just their cause. The pure-hearted contend that such an attitude is lacking in nobility, and difficult to defend on the moral plane. True enough. But the mandarinate knows that uncertain or lost causes mean trouble. They put no money into anyone's pocket, nor do they lead to advancement for those who defend them. It's better to team up with the winners and the powerful, instead of splitting hairs.

∞ ∞ ∞

All lies are not right to tell, sighs the senior bureaucrat.

When a senior bureaucrat asks you to speak frankly, it means he has already started lying to you. Do not be so imprudent as to accept his invitation, for he will classify you among the naive individuals of this world — or, worse, among the imbeciles. The least you can do to avoid disappointing him and losing his respect is to lie to him. That's what he expects. Go ahead, he'll smile . . . You'll get along just fine.

∞ ∞ ∞

Sometimes, a senior public servant will lie badly, damaging his own reputation and that of his caste. Either through weariness, lack of intelligence, or a lowering of his professional standards, he will let himself go. The resulting negligence can spell disaster for him. In some cases, the trouble springs from a poor quality lie, which betrays a serious failing in imagination and judgement. Other times, the lie veers dangerously close to the improbable. Perhaps the culprit is an absence of perspective or chronology, sorely straining the mandarin's credibility with his audience. Some of his lies even have built-in construction faults, which an experienced mind can detect and, if ever it should come to that, even prove, exposing the mandarin's lie in the process. The result is a sullying of all and sundry, the individual mandarin and all his kind.

Other times, errors due to failing memory or a lack of vigilance occur. The mind's tension momentarily relaxes, and distractions successfully take root there. Things begin to unravel. The senior public servant suddenly loses sight — all it takes is an instant — of the continuum that a lie needs to develop and reach maturity. Variations may appear, especially if the lie is used at an interval of several weeks. The situation can be saved, if the differences can be passed off as details, or additional, supplementary explanations added to the first version. But if they are not well controlled and managed, if they overflow the borders of continuity and logic, if they blatantly display contradictory faces, then matters are more serious. The author of the lie may be accused of cooking the books. And once again, the entire tribe of the mandarinate will be tarred with the same brush.

Lying is a powerful and effective weapon, but to use it successfully, the user must know how to handle it and its dangers. Never attempt to use it if you are not in full possession of your means, either temporarily or permanently. A word of warning to senior public servants who are not always, nor not even often, in control of theirs.

∞ ∞ ∞

Between the Mob and the mandarinate, the difference is not so great. The main one is this: the latter does not use firearms and hates the sight of blood. That's about all there is . . .

∞ ∞ ∞

The bureaucracy is like a gaming house. Are you going to stand there on the doorstep like a prudent child, or are you going to go inside and learn to play these endless games, in which everyone wants to beat the rules? Come on, relax, throw your dice. Who knows what will happen?

∞ ∞ ∞

Have you ever noticed that a senior bureaucrat never blushes? That gives you an idea of his level of conscience . . . or lack thereof. But his insensitivity and impassiveness are perhaps not such a bad thing. Because if he were to blush according to each of his thoughts and deeds, he would surely appear to have a large strawberry birthmark.

∞ ∞ ∞

The senior public servant knows perfectly well that, under the table, Old Nick and our Lord are holding hands.

∞ ∞ ∞

Like his master the politician, the senior bureaucrat understands that his personal advancement must take precedence over the public good. Of course, he can never admit this. He must pretend that such an abject thought never even grazed his conscience. But let him forget this rule even an instant and a colleague, apparently as virtuous as he is, will slip silently past him. That, too, he knows.

∞ ∞ ∞

Mandarins are great atheists. Everything they do presupposes that time stops here, on earth, forever and ever, and they will never have to answer for their actions in the theoretical Great Beyond. Besides, if ever it turns out they were wrong, they know they can count on God's clemency and forgiveness. And, who can say, perhaps on his complicity as well. But, in the meantime, a bird in the hand is worth two in the bush.

∞ ∞ ∞

The senior bureaucrat shows his collection of white canes to close friends only.

∞ ∞ ∞

Antiquity speaks to us of princes and judges enamoured of honesty and justice, and so absolutely moral that they displayed more care, rigour and impartiality than usual when, in some cause, a family member or a friend was involved, interceding in favour of a third party or advancing a particular solution. The senior public servant and the modern judge belong to another civilization. They follow a less demanding code. Instinctively, they distrust anything they perceive as an excess, a transport, an intransigence in the administration of justice and application of moral values. Their sense of compromise is so potent it can make good and evil cohabit and cut deals, manoeuvre the most extreme positions into touching, and in the most varied and numerous ways. Just as, in the circus, sometimes, we may notice a brown bear, absent-minded, nonchalant, mounting an impassive horse.

∞ ∞ ∞

Alas, the face of corruption in the top levels of bureaucracy is quite real. It is as ugly, contemptible and commonplace as they say it is. It is also very well concealed. So well that, each time it affects or hurts you personally, you feel as if you've been assaulted or violated by the Invisible Man.

∞ ∞ ∞

Cries of horror and protest. A top mandarin was caught red-handed in the governmental cookie jar! He has been accused of falsifying the bidding process, personally benefitting from the sale of public property, meddling in secret files, hiring friends and family, and that's just the start of it . . . Infamy is attached to his name, his career has been compromised, he has discredited the entire race of senior bureaucrats. Not because he was immoral and dishonest. He just wasn't clever enough not to get caught.

∞ ∞ ∞

The senior bureaucrat has no need for the Mob to do his dirty work. He can do it very well himself, thank you.

∞ ∞ ∞

Never plagiarize a senior public servant. If you do, you may end up being accused of plagiarism by a third party.

∞ ∞ ∞

With the passage of time, the mandarinate has developed a set of morals particular to them, somewhat outside those subscribed to by the rest of society. The way prisoners adopt an ethic of their own, which may astonish, amuse or even offend the ordinary citizen. Which explains the periodic appearance of corpses, though the forces of this particular justice are never found. They apply a code known to them alone, and only they know the secret reasons that push them to action.

∞ ∞ ∞

Some people have a quite abusive attitude toward our poor senior bureaucrats, demanding they display excessive qualities and virtues, which are much too heavy for their frail shoulders. They would be crushed under the weight of notions such as truth, goodness, honesty, justice, intelligence, loyalty, etc. There is no chance they could have come up against such concepts during their brief stay at university — certainly not in their accounting or economics courses — nor could they have learned them during their time on the front lines in the inferior positions they occupied for so many years. When it comes to these notions, the bureaucracy is not demanding; it will take pot luck. It believes in the theory of the noble savage. It also believes that one can't simply learn certain notions, that a person is born with a collection of virtues and qualities, just as we come into this world with the requisite number of fingers and toes, and that virtues and qualities develop well or poorly, depending on the caprices of random chance and the individual's idiosyncracies. The bureaucracy maintains that, if you're a little competent or a little virtuous, that's virtuous and competent enough. The important things are elsewhere.

∞ ∞ ∞

A certain mandarin of our acquaintance is unconsolable: unlike his private sector colleagues, he cannot make use of the many legal pretexts to reduce his taxes. He cannot even employ any of those little white lies others enjoy to defraud the taxman. Because, you see, more than anyone else, as a public servant he is subject to an easy, quick and ineluctable check on his revenue. But, there is balm. At least he can prevent the largest possible number of dishonest businessmen from using the many loopholes the system provides.

∞ ∞ ∞

At Christmas, the ministry's top mandarin organized an intimate little wine and cheese party in his office. Besides his inner staff, he invited the most influential of his bureaucrats. One of them enticed a secretary, who had taken a glass or two too many, onto a pink couch, where he fornicated with her as his colleagues looked the other way.

After it was over, the secretary recovered her senses, and began crying. They all did their best to console her. Some time later, she submitted her resignation and left the ministry. The affair, which had never been the stuff of gossip, was completely forgotten.

∞ ∞ ∞

The senior public servant will not do it, unless he is assured of complete impunity. Then he is ready for anything.

∞ ∞ ∞

The mandarin will gladly lie when the lie appears truer than the truth. On the other hand, he speaks the truth when it seems truer than the lie. The important thing is to deceive as well as possible.

∞ ∞ ∞

If you look long and hard, you can always find a senior bureaucrat who has never knowingly been dishonest. But to find one who has been dishonest only once is a much rarer thing.

∞ ∞ ∞

Contrary to public opinion, actually an affectionate and indulgent joke, grand and fatal flaws are not limited to great men. Senior public servants have them as well.

∞ ∞ ∞

The fine accomplishments of the mandarinate are like sausages. It is better to live in ignorance of what's inside, and not wonder why you never find them on the butcher's plate. For the truth may lead to nausea.

∞ ∞ ∞

The senior public servant has no need to correct yesterday's errors. As long as they have shown their worth and served him well in the past.

∞ ∞ ∞

The senior bureaucracy provides an excellent contrast with the exasperatingly traditional American cowboy film, in which the good guys win and the bad guys are punished. It comes as something of a relief to see the slow, incompetent shooters hit the target, too.

∞ ∞ ∞

The senior bureaucrat never turns to blackmail, lies or theft to obtain what he covets free of charge. At his disposal, he has other means both more efficient and infinitely more discreet.

∞ ∞ ∞

For the member of the mandarinate, being right or wrong is secondary. The name of the game is to win. By what means? By whatever means possible, of course! Except those that might awaken the suspicions of journalists and lead him to the witness stand . . . His preferred methods are those that preserve and advertise his reputation for serene objectivity and rock-hard integrity.

∞ ∞ ∞

For the senior bureaucrat, lying is not a simple, ordinary procedure. On the contrary. A lie is always colourful, dressed to the nines, in its Sunday best, decorated with ribbons and medals. Depending on the circumstance, it appeals to diplomacy, which demands all kinds of adjustments and compromises. It insists on official secrecy, which has its own hidden imperatives. On professional obligation, which conjures up the code of solidarity among ranking members of the hierarchy. On authority, which needs not explain nor render an accounting. On administrative difficulties, which presents an inexhaustable choice of convincing and uncheckable explanations and excuses. On savoir-vivre, which allows one to twist the truth ever so slightly to lubricate the wheel of social relations. On forgetting and even amnesia, which are always plausible, acceptable reasons, given the thousands of preoccupations and details that assault the senior public servant's mind on a daily basis . . .

Of course, the goal is always the same: the intent to deceive. But coming from the mouth of the mandarin, a lie — and we insist upon this vulgar term — takes on a kind of dimension and volume that overtakes the teller. It reaches a kind of particular elegance, authority and sonority. It is the most perfect example of the new humanism inspired by the world of top management.

∞ ∞ ∞

The senior bureaucrat has always known this simple truth: like the street-walker, justice can be had for a price. But he can't always afford fine flesh. Some days, he has to settle for less.

∞ ∞ ∞

For the mandarin, justice is an unpleasant accident along the road of his career, an obstacle to be skirted, lost time to be made up. Fortunately, there are many roads to his goal.

∞ ∞ ∞

Justice will lie down with only the best lawyers.

∞ ∞ ∞

The nightmare is not that there is no God and no Devil. The horror is that, in their absence, there will be no one to demand an accounting of the mandarinate. And no Purgatory or Hell to receive their souls.

∞ ∞ ∞

A certain judge we know always fancied his young administrative assistant, who happened to be a woman, as well as being efficient and pleasant. He went to the bureaucrat whose job it is to fill new positions and insisted that he promote her. But to no avail: the bureaucrat had his scruples. He hesitated. He was married to the rule book. He was also stubborn and, though he did not clearly and definitively refuse to appoint the favoured assistant, he put off the decision so long that the whole business began to fester. What's all this talk about competitions, and merit principle, and administrative norms? Didn't the judge himself examine and weigh everything and come to a decision? What more could anyone want? Who would dare ask for more?

Exasperated, the judge set aside his usual impartiality and went right to the root of the problem. He called a lady friend of his, who happened to hold a high rank in the Public Service, and who also happened to be the boss of this intractable bureaucrat. The lady solved the problem in the usual friendly fashion: she reassigned this scupulous underling and named a more understanding bureaucrat in his place. The latter official wasted no time finding the correct loophole in the labyrinth of rules and regulations, and justified the judge's decision. His will was done. He was free to choose the assistant he desired above all others.

The affair was settled in the wink of an eye. After months and months of administrative foot-dragging, the judge and his newly promoted assistant drove off together in a black limousine, en route to the Courthouse, legitimately seated on real chestnut-coloured leather seat covers. They are on their way to hear a famous case (all the papers are talking about it), involving a company president accused of fraud and influence peddling.

"What a sordid business," the judge remarks. "Today's world is filled with abuse of power and corruption. Fortunately we are here to redress the situation, and hold high the flame of justice . . ."

∞ ∞ ∞

Lack of success, weariness and discouragement often lead the senior public servant back to integrity, truth and the straight-and-narrow.

"What's the use?" he says to himself, resignation in his voice. "I'll never make it."

∞ ∞ ∞

The senior bureaucrat lies best when he says or does nothing at all. And lies most, too. When he watches someone make a mistake without pointing it out to him. When he lets a deadline go by without getting involved. When he drops a few sentences in a document he is quoting. When he doesn't call back as promised. When he changes the subject just as the conversation is reaching the heart of the matter. When he sticks to the facts, then stops short of saying what the facts imply.

These attenuated forms of lying are kinder to his conscience. They allow him the illusion of integrity. They assure him of his skills as a clever diplomat.

∞ ∞ ∞

Do not be offended if the senior bureaucrat displays more indulgence toward himself than toward others. He is in sorer need of forgiveness than the rest of us. We will get along just fine.

∞ ∞ ∞

The mandarin knows there is no more dangerous way to lie than with words, for morals and convention can combine to confound and judge the liar. The sentencing that must surely follow allows of no appeal, since the sin committed was vulgar, low-class, without imagination or elegance. Everyone knows that an ugly sin is much more serious, infinitely more reprehensible than an ordinary sin.

On the other hand, the mandarin knows he can lie with impunity by using the body's language and eloquence, especially what the face can be made to express. Gestures, gazes, movements of the head, even the lack of movement — the universe of non-verbal expression — can become a powerful, infallible way of lying. Safety is assured. He knows he has crossed those invisible limits beyond which human subtlety cannot go, where lawyers, judges and courts refuse to venture, where proof fades like the stars at dawn, where punishment is hardly ever justified, where lies become matters of diverse, opposing and troubling interpretations. The senior public servant knows he has reached the uncertain, outer borders where no one can say where fiction ends and reality begins. In that land of precarious equilibrium, his talent comes to its full flowering.

∞ ∞ ∞

The ideal universe does not exist. Good can flourish only if it is accompanied by an imperfect reality that is its support and well-spring. Just as colour can be manifest only through material medium: the pulp of an orange, the flesh of an amaryllis, the texture of a sponge, the fibre of paper. Of course, the senior public servant is not really aware of all that. But in some confused manner, in his own way, he has understood it quite perfectly.

∞ ∞ ∞

Members of the mandarinate who would condemn and despise the bank robber would have no qualms about making off with a fine bottle of wine bought for an official reception. The difference between them and the robber is not one of principle, but of courage. Petty courage, petty theft. Senior public servants don't have the stuff to become high-profile, internationally known criminals. Even perversity can be lacking in grandeur.

18
Virtues

~❦~

At the heart of the world, on the heart of the world is injustice, this giant lupus clinging to its living flesh. The senior bureaucrat sees but is not alarmed. Like a fast and skillful player, like a flat stone skipping across the water, he takes his share of its profits, he makes it part of his game. Meanwhile, ordinary people stand motionless, transfixed by the monster.

∞ ∞ ∞

The senior public servant knows that justice and truth are not of this world. And so he rubs his hands with glee, ready to benefit to the fullest from the occasion.

∞ ∞ ∞

The mandarin's motto: it is better to receive than to give.

∞ ∞ ∞

In the upper-echelon bureaucracy, lovers of justice and truth are wet blankets who disturb an otherwise orderly universe. They constitute living proof of the excesses that spring from all forms of intransigent virtue. Whereas career bureaucrats instinctively prefer agreements made under the table, whispered conversations, friendly solutions, late-afternoon phone calls, backroom handshakes, successfully concluded negotiations on the stairway, têtes-à-têtes among peers, secretly shared weekends, exchanges of little services, strongly recommended secretaries, family resemblances, and the thousand slippery forms of nuance and compromise.

∞ ∞ ∞

Among the mandarinate, the natural tendency toward good-ness, honesty and justice continues, despite what others say. If the senior public servant does not quite reach these ideals, it's only because they demand a certain quality of being that he can rarely lay claim to. Contrary to what most people think, just by wishing to be good, honest or just does not ensure you are these things. It's been said before: there is no such thing as easy virtue.

∞ ∞ ∞

Senior bureaucrats serve the government and nation with superhuman, admirable, tireless devotion. They are willing to continue doing so as long as they are needed, come what may . . . That is, as long as we have the means to pay them, both generously and at regular intervals.

∞ ∞ ∞

When a mandarin stops pretending he's working, you know he must have very good reasons.

∞ ∞ ∞

As long as his personal situation is not at stake, the senior bureaucrat is prepared to make any arrangement, any accom-modation, any compromise. He is willing to commit any treason or crime of the spirit. But since a goodly number of his colleagues offer the exact same service, rivalry is strong and competition tough. Clients are not always easy to find. The senior public serv-ant becomes a sin waiting to be committed. Like the convent girl ready to sacrifice her chastity, behind the walls where even the gardener is a woman. Desire and consent are present, but the opportunity is horribly lacking.

∞ ∞ ∞

In the higher zones of the bureaucracy, justice is like a virgin defended by the impotent. Along comes a virile specimen who takes her, body and soul. The impotent, who had temporarily dispersed, return to her side. They will help her give birth to a fine bouncing baby.

∞ ∞ ∞

Justice and truth are potions too hot and powerful for our senior public servant. Instinctively, he waters them down.

∞ ∞ ∞

A certain member of the mandarinate has acquired complete self-control when it comes to suffering. Other people's suffering, of course.

∞ ∞ ∞

If you appeal to his sense of honour in an attempt to convince a senior public servant to do something, you will catch him completely off guard. When he recovers his wits again, he will ask himself, immediately and instinctively, how he can benefit from such an original concept which, he must admit, never crossed his mind before.

∞ ∞ ∞

When the mandarin gets worse, no one notices. Not until he starts getting better does it become noticeable. It's exactly like getting one's ears frostbitten.

∞ ∞ ∞

Why is the certain senior bureaucrat so willing to make concessions, consent to accommodations, even tolerate dubious dealings with other men? He does not want to be left alone with Virtue, this poor, sad, ugly little girl who never seduced a single heart.

∞ ∞ ∞

Since they are honourable, fair-minded men, senior public servants avoid being associated, even at a distance, with vulgar injustices that stir the people, scandalize them, make the headlines. Yet they are brimming with understanding, forgiveness, even tenderness for the charming little injustices that make life so pleasant and relations so easy, that add that social lubricant to a difficult negotiation. You know the motto: what they don't know won't hurt them.

Don't be surprised if you hear one of them say to his colleague, "What's your nephew's name again? Tell him to come see me. It just so happens I need an assistant."

∞ ∞ ∞

Whatever else happens, a mandarin always has clean hands.

∞ ∞ ∞

Among senior bureaucrats, sincerity is often just a purified, refined form of a lie. The former is the butterfly; the latter is still in the larval stage. But whatever the appearance, you are still dealing with the same insect.

∞ ∞ ∞

A senior public servant makes a public profession of honesty and sincerity; do not be taken in. He's just trying to convince you of the opposite of what he suspects he is, and convince himself in the process. His image, the one he displays to himself, is like a raging fire continually consuming him.

∞ ∞ ∞

The integrity of the mandarinate is like the yeti. Everyone talks about it, but no one can offer an eye-witness account.

∞ ∞ ∞

The senior bureaucrats who read this book may laugh out loud, amused, perhaps, and charmed, too. "These are just caricatures, the mischievous sayings of a punster . . ." Not so. They are the plain truth.

∞ ∞ ∞

Senior public servants practise their sincerity and honesty, the way others do a half-hour of scales every day or thirty lengths in the pool.

∞ ∞ ∞

Since the top bureaucrat is never punished, he soon believes he is always right. And since he believes he is always right, he is sure he never does anything wrong. And if he never does anything wrong, why would he be punished?

An example of circular bureaucratic thinking.

∞ ∞ ∞

The mandarin actually does believe in himself. Therein lies the tragedy.

∞ ∞ ∞

The senior bureaucrat knows he can get himself into serious trouble by striving for perfect honesty, justice, sincerity, accuracy, devotion and truth. Virtue in its extreme form is a kind of disequilibrium. It betrays a lack of maturity and wisdom. He avoids it as if it were vice itself.

∞ ∞ ∞

The mandarin's nightmare: that one day he will be called upon to present his own defence, in person, before a real court, subject to justice as administered by someone else. From time to time he himself must act as judge, but he has neither the taste nor the talent to be the accused, or even a witness. He will do anything, including going back on a decision he made regarding a subordinate, to avoid the public tribunal and the ordinary justice that is every citizen's right.

"There are at least two kinds of justice," says the mandarin. "Bureaucratic justice, and the court's justice. The two should not be confused."

The senior public servant is a thousand percent correct. The justice of the courts is direct, objective, stripped bare, while the bureacratic kind is, more often than not, charged with a complex mission that varies according to the case at hand. It can be merciful, vengeful, compensatory, exemplary, disciplinary, conciliatory, strategic, etc. This species of justice goes beyond simple virtue to become a flexible management tool, both secretive and personal. Only the senior public servant's impromptu decision determines its nature, for that particular day, for that specific hour, for that fleeting moment . . .

∞ ∞ ∞

A senior public servant is furious with someone. He is tempted to overtly display his wrath, but he stops himself. Instead, he will eliminate the slightest affiliation, correlation or causality that might be established between the anger he feels and any action he might take, even the least consequential. If even a shadow of a doubt remains, he may be accused of lacking maturity, being unable to rein in his emotions, incapable of facing stressful situations. Little by little, calm returns. And everyone forgets the incident.

Except the senior public servant . . . When enough time has elapsed since his initial anger, and everyone's attention is focussed elsewhere, only then will he move, carrying out his cold act of vengeance, giving his calm, methodical anger free rein.

∞ ∞ ∞

Take this member of the mandarinate. He employed so much skill, cleverness and patience at his deception that we can't quite summon up the courage to tell him that his plans have been foiled. We can't bring ourselves to blow down such a carefully constructed edifice. It would be like telling an innocent child that Santa Claus is really Daddy.

∞ ∞ ∞

Virtue and integrity, among the mandarinate, often result from a lack of opportunity, or some stubborn piece of bad luck that keeps him from acting freely. He is compelled to walk the straight-and-narrow.

∞ ∞ ∞

If necessary, the mandarin can display modesty. As long as someone notices and appreciates it. But in general, he stays clear of hidden virtues that bring no obvious, measurable, quantifiable benefit.

∞ ∞ ∞

Like farm animals in winter, senior bureaucrats find the heat and comfort necessary to their existence in their own tight circle. An advantage, of course. Yet it isolates them and makes them insensitive to outside opinion, and impervious to the feelings they inspire in others. Even if you could inform them of this, and they could understand you, they would be just as astonished as the people of Berlin were, when the Allies stormed their city, to learn of the hatred the very name of the German nation conjured up in the hearts of the world.

∞ ∞ ∞

We know of a certain senior bureaucrat who displays such a natural falseness that we end up accepting it, even if it does irritate or discomfort us. We grow accustomed to him, as we would to his near-sightedness, or the wart on his chin.

Kindness comes suddenly to the mandarin. It falls like a warm, unexpected spring shower, brought on by an attack of maturity. For the first time in his life, he discovers this new dimension as through a split in a rock face, as he gazes down upon the agonies of the bureaucracy. Goodness knocks him off his donkey like Paul struck down by divine light on the road to Damascus. He brims over with new-found grace. To prove his recent virtue, to show the reborn man within, he orders one of his friends named to a new position, immediately, without taking the usual precautions or even preparing a fall-back position should difficulties arise. Simply out of goodness, to spare his friend the worry and humiliation of the usual competition, so deadening and unworthy for people of quality, who are so obviously meritorious that they need not prove it.

∞ ∞ ∞

There is a kind of resignation and defeatism in the way the senior public servant goes about using the schemes he knows by heart. They are good for every occasion, and let him bend the long, monotonous line of regulations as he wishes, leap them as in an obstacle race. At the beginning, he, too had his virginity. But by now, he has had every experience, seen it all, he derives no further pleasure from disobedience or trickery. Just like a woman who has grown accustomed to the business of making love, who has long since abandoned any search for romance or even eroticism in the act, who muses on the colour of the ceiling while her partner finally achieves his long sought-for spasm of pleasure.

∞ ∞ ∞

The senior bureaucrat discovered long ago that modesty is nothing else than the art of letting others find out just how powerful and influential he is.

∞ ∞ ∞

The mandarin's constant level-headedness, quietude and balance flow less from the faculty of judgement, maturity and self-control than from indifference, boredom, lethargy. For him, virtue is but another form of absence.

∞ ∞ ∞

If you are naive enough to swear fealty to a senior bureaucrat, then you deserve the infidelity he will display toward you, when the occasion calls for it. Instead, choose disloyalty; you will be closer to him.

∞ ∞ ∞

The senior bureaucrat has no truck with wisdom, for it is a virtue that belongs to old men, the weak of spirit and losers.

∞ ∞ ∞

The mandarin positions himself well within the truth, but in such a way as to extend its domain and grant it new and unexpected dimensions. Discreetly and imperceptibly — as the sea erodes the shore — it will encroach upon uncertainty, exaggeration, hypothesis, presumption, chance, probability, unlikely appearances, hesitation, etc.

∞ ∞ ∞

A certain senior bureaucrat enjoys being disturbed in his work. It is his way of idling away the time, without the unpleasantness of remorse.

∞ ∞ ∞

Among the mandarinate, goodness is simply ambition in repose.

∞ ∞ ∞

The senior bureaucrat knows that the best is difficult to reach, and does not endure. So he opts for the next best.

To be modest, one must first be innocent, which is beyond the senior bureaucrat. At best, he displays the modesty of someone who feigns innocence.

∞ ∞ ∞

The senior bureaucrat makes mistakes with authority and aplomb. Well, too bad for the truth!

∞ ∞ ∞

Among the upper-level bureaucrats, the need for diplomacy and strategy destroys any impulse to sincerity or honesty. In this strange race, qualities win out over virtues.

∞ ∞ ∞

I cannot stand the honesty of the senior public servant. It is more calculated than virtuous.

∞ ∞ ∞

Sincerity, among the mandarinate, is but a momentary weakness. Soon, the crisis will be over.

∞ ∞ ∞

For the senior bureaucratic body, truth, goodness, justice and the entire string of sweet little virtues are like the garish, ingenious road signs that line the edges of our highways. They inform, they advise, they exhort, but they will never stop a single driver who has decided to ignore them and speed on.

∞ ∞ ∞

The senior bureaucrat gives just enough to be satisfied with himself, and achieve a clear conscience. It is the only case in which giving is, for him, better than receiving.

Justice is so dreadfully boring, says the mandarin. Like a pretty woman who is so intransigently virtuous that she will not bestow as much as a smile on anyone, and who takes stubborn refuge in distant, inaccessible austerity. Besides, the administration of justice does not call for particularly remarkable qualities. One must know and apply the elementary rules and principles, trusting one's common sense and judgement that Nature generously gave most human beings.

But the practice of injustice is much more difficult. For starters, one must reject the comfortable and convenient principles and rules that give daily life its routine quality, and remove the need to think too much. Injustice puts you into situations wherein no law prevails. You must continually seek your own path in the threatening jungle of endless possibilties. Find a precarious and unstable balance, and maintain it. Avoid the many dangers that could cause terminal accidents. Yet this choice procures you secret joys of an unspeakable intensity. You are no longer subject to morality's insipid codes, you are truly free to swim and float in moral space, with a wave of your hand you cast aside logic, you set your own limits yourself, your personal will is your only sure criterion.

You say: run this red light, and you run it. You say: make this steel beam float, and it floats. Discreetly eliminate this person from my organization, and he disappears. Name a friend you met in Montreal to this position, and he gets the job. Change this bureaucrat into a hen, and he begins to cackle. Get rid of this bag lady, and it is done. What an enchanting universe, misshapen and skittish, where injustice is a magnificent caprice and an endless pleasure.

∞ ∞ ∞

When the senior bureaucrat displays his goodness, he knows he could just as well display the opposite tendency, if it pleased him. Otherwise, he wouldn't take the risk.

∞ ∞ ∞

The mandarin knows full well that if ever justice and truth were to conspire against him to defeat him in the theatre of battle, he need only cast power into the fray, and the issue would be his. Of course, the victory would be less refined and noble, but not less real. And that's what matters.

∞ ∞ ∞

Any virtue that does not contribute to the senior bureaucrat's reputation, his influence or advancement, is a vice in disguise.

∞ ∞ ∞

The forgiving mandarin is a watchful mandarin.

∞ ∞ ∞

After a lifetime struggle, the aging senior public servant re-signs himself to wisdom. As others of the same age learn to accept slowness of hand, weakness of limb, or disease.

∞ ∞ ∞

The senior bureaucrat will gladly extend his mercy when there is no further use in prolonging the pain.

∞ ∞ ∞

The mandarin will see justice done if necessary, but as a last resort, and only if there is no other solution . . . Even though he swore to himself he'd never get caught in that impasse again.

∞ ∞ ∞

An honest senior bureaucrat is one who displays integrity and loyalty when dealing with his accomplices.

∞ ∞ ∞

When they come into contact with the mandarinate, princi-ples and virtues are worn down, they lose their cutting edge, grow dull and wear away. Honesty begins to cut deals, respect takes on the face of mockery, justice discovers untapped sources of flexibility, loyalty learns how to wink, secrets escape into the air like volatile gas, fidelity learns to live with minor indiscretions, trust is tainted with mistrust. Welcome to a universe without right angles and sharp corners, without perpendicularity. Welcome to a universe of rounded, slippery curves, soft grades, gentle slopes, and the ease of quick surfaces.

∞ ∞ ∞

Among the mandarinate, routine, regularity, repetition, monotony and custom appear as qualities and virtues. We always end up enjoying and appreciating that which constrains and makes us suffer, as hostages in the modern age of terrorism come to espouse and defend their captors' cause.

∞ ∞ ∞

The senior public servant has mastered the art of not speaking the truth without openly lying. Or, in any case, without anyone being able to catch him at it. No one has ever perfected this art to such a degree, except diplomats, perhaps, who, like politicians, obviously and brazenly lie, without taking any precautions to hide or deny, and without their reputations or credit suffering. The reason? Lying goes beyond the lowly moral order of things to become an effective but ordinary way of negotiating and exerting pressure. By a kind of transcendence, lying reaches the status of an official institution, respectable and respected, contributing to the enrichment of Western civilization.

19
Qualities

What makes a man a great public servant is the very thing that prevents him from becoming a great man.

∞ ∞ ∞

The senior bureaucrat uses logic the way a blind man uses his cane, tracing the path that seems to have the fewest obstacles. It may also be that, accidentally, the truth is lurking nearby.

∞ ∞ ∞

Behind the mandarin's apparent weakness is concealed a real one.

∞ ∞ ∞

We may be too demanding of our senior bureaucrats. Perhaps we are entrusting them with too great a responsibility, and expecting of them performances which are beyond their means, their human machine being incapable of reaching such excessively high standards. Like certain types of airplanes that are not designed to fly at too high an altitude, withstand too quick a rate of acceleration, or go beyond a given speed without breaking up. In fact, most senior bureaucrats still fly like the Wright brothers.

∞ ∞ ∞

The mandarin's qualities are also his prison. Without them, he would go further and higher, perhaps. But he is held back by a lesser perfection.

∞ ∞ ∞

To each problem, there is a solution. The difficulty is in finding it. Of course, the senior bureaucrat would be the last person able to do so, but he bravely continues plodding on.

∞ ∞ ∞

Senior bureaucrats are like beautiful women who, at first glance, seem like formidable strongboxes which you can enter only by breaking down the door. Then look at them more closely: they are, indeed, formidable strongboxes. But the door has been left open and anything inside that might have been precious has long since been rifled. Containers are almost always more durable than their contents.

∞ ∞ ∞

The law of heredity states that all of a child's undesirable characteristics come from whichever of its two parents was a bureaucrat. When both share this profession, pity the child . . . It's best not to think of the results.

∞ ∞ ∞

Deputy Ministers are like bulls. Their intelligence, perseverance and competence do not account for the respect we show them. Instead, beware of their weight, their momentum and that natural tendency they have to be on top of the herd.

∞ ∞ ∞

Like everyone else, senior bureaucrats catch colds. But rarely do they catch head colds.

∞ ∞ ∞

The senior public servant's brilliance is akin to that of a flash-bulb, rather than that of a lamp. His brief light blinds rather than illuminates, and never is his exploit repeated. The darkness that follows seems to last forever.

∞ ∞ ∞

The mandarin uses the word "philosophy" with bitterness and derision, knowing it applies to a higher universe from which he is excluded. The same distance stands between the philosopher and the bureaucrat as between the eagle and the sparrow. But there are many more sparrows than eagles.

∞ ∞ ∞

To improve their bodies' productivity, senior bureaucrats turn to glasses, hearing aids, false teeth, crutches and a thousand other prostheses. Except for that part of themselves they abuse most constantly, which is clearly the most solid of their members: the one upon which they sit.

∞ ∞ ∞

A senior public servant does not require much. He is happy with very little. He practises mental thriftiness. A tiny crumb of thought suffices.

∞ ∞ ∞

The mandarin, the only chameleon that has the ability to change colour, yet is colour-blind. Or at least he believes he is, given the greyness of his world.

∞ ∞ ∞

Despite his desperate efforts to persuade himself of his own worth, the senior bureaucrat never quite succeeds. Except if he is completely stupid. But then he doesn't succeed in convincing anyone else.

The sitting position, which has been adopted and perfected by the mandarinate since the dawn of time, is a clear improvement on the upright posture of the ordinary primate. It cuts down on wind resistance, lessens the risk of injury from a fall, provides more headroom in automobiles, reduces absenteeism caused by aching feet, and makes use of the strong parts of the human skeleton. Had he paused to think about it, Darwin might have been more inclined to a vision of a squatting humanity.

∞ ∞ ∞

The highest form of expression among the mandarinate is silence. When it isn't, it should be.

∞ ∞ ∞

The senior bureaucrat attains the level he can. As the feeble-minded display whatever intelligence they can. In both cases, we are seized with compassion.

∞ ∞ ∞

Label on a senior public servant: sensitive to light.

∞ ∞ ∞

Ever since his promotion, the senior bureaucrat feels his IQ has grown appreciably.

∞ ∞ ∞

Among the mandarinate, mind and intelligence graze the surface, but remain submerged. Still, we feel that a little more effort, the smallest push, and they would break through and flower like black water lilies. Within us, hope is rekindled.

∞ ∞ ∞

If you happen to be near a senior bureaucrat who is thinking, listen closely. You may hear a slight humming, like that of an electric motor, or a fan, perhaps. What? You don't believe me . . . Then it's obvious you've never seen a member of the mandarinate in the act of reflection . . . Yes, I agree, you have to be patient, but luck will help . . . It's a little bit like finding a four-leafed clover.

∞ ∞ ∞

Nature usually creates the form to fit the function. Thus, the physical attributes of the senior bureaucrat are perfectly suited to what he is and what he does. Unfortunately, there is nothing anyone can do about it.

∞ ∞ ∞

Never let a senior bureaucrat defend your interests. A brilliant defence is more important to him than a true defence.

∞ ∞ ∞

Long ago, the mandarin understood that fine qualities like hope, courage, ambition, ingenuity, enthusiasm and energy are all vanquished sooner or later by a superior force that he himself has mastered, and which is called, among other names, immobility, inertia, stasis, inaction, stagnation, paralysis. This force triumphs through erosion, destroying everything that comes into contact with it in the hope of supplanting it.

∞ ∞ ∞

A certain senior bureaucrat is completely useless. But he plays the role to the hilt, with authority and conviction.

∞ ∞ ∞

Don't try to understand what this mandarin is explaining to you for the third time. Just continue giving him your polite attention.

It is impossible to be sure of a senior bureaucrat's IQ. On the other hand, it is easy to tell what it is not.

∞ ∞ ∞

At times, the senior public servant will speak out of both sides of his mouth. Fortunately, his partner in conversation rarely senses it. Or if he does, he sees it as a kind of continuity, a sort of natural, logical flow with the rest of his speech.

∞ ∞ ∞

Don't waste your time describing a senior bureaucrat's qualities and praising them to his face. He already knows all that.

∞ ∞ ∞

All human beings have hidden qualities. Senior public servants have more than others. Some of their qualities are so well hidden that no one has ever discovered them.

∞ ∞ ∞

The reputations of some senior bureaucrats grow because of their faults, not their qualities. This is fair and reasonable. It is normal to achieve fame for what one excels in.

∞ ∞ ∞

Often, when they speak, senior bureaucrats open an imaginary verbal parenthesis and never close it. At times they open two or three in a row, without closing a single one. The listener may find this phenomenon curious but, all things considered, it is little more than a problem of punctuation. But what perplexes and confuses him is the sequence and logic of the mandarin's speech. That is, unless the person listening is another senior bureaucrat, in which case he finds nothing out of the ordinary.

∞ ∞ ∞

To become a senior public servant, you must know how to take advantage of everything you are, not just your qualities.

∞ ∞ ∞

When a member of the mandarinate, in an act of friendship, takes you into his confidence and purposely displays his foibles, be assured that he has chosen the most flattering among them, the ones that put him in the best light, though foibles they may be, in the process diverting you from his other faults that might tarnish his image in your eyes. He may proudly tell you how he tricked his provincial counterpart by giving him obsolete or incomplete data, but conveniently forget about the permanent loan he took of the new portable calculator purchased by his office.

∞ ∞ ∞

The most profound aspect of the senior bureaucrat is the line between his two buttocks. If that's not it, it must be somewhere nearby.

∞ ∞ ∞

Without being defeatist, the senior bureaucrat is a realist and knows where his limits lie. That is why he seeks excellence where he can find it, and requires perfection in others only.

∞ ∞ ∞

We naturally associate wisdom with experience and age, and generally assume it is the final step of a person's development, the point at which he attains his highest perfection and deepest self-knowledge. Wisdom is one among the many resources the mandarin has, a component of his overall strategy, one of the arrows in his quiver. If it fails to procure him what he wants, he will reject it and turn to means more direct and more energetic. So much for negotiation, conciliation and diplomacy. So much for good sense, morality and maturity. In short, so much for wisdom.

In hopes of gaining some advantage, the senior bureaucrat will work to acquire a foible he has noticed and admires in a colleague. Yet he will avoid being influenced by that same colleague's qualities, which may be worthwhile but hardly likely to lead to present or future profit.

∞ ∞ ∞

The senior public servant has no use for those qualities whose effects and benefits emerge over the long term. His sense of the immediate comes quickly to the fore and puts a quick end to any hazy speculations. He grows summer cabbages rather than winter ones.

∞ ∞ ∞

Among the mandarinate, a calculus is more often a problem in the kidneys than an operation of the mind.

∞ ∞ ∞

The senior bureaucrat distrusts those who, like Christmas trees loaded with decorations of every colour and shape, bristle with a thousand qualities and virtues. He knows that those people will only produce insipid goods. In his eyes, modern man, or, at least, the mandarin in the making, is one who presents a good mixture of qualities and faults, virtues and weaknesses, which together produce a dynamic and productive balance.

∞ ∞ ∞

The senior public servant has trouble separating repose from idleness, and is not quite sure if his body or his mind is at issue.

∞ ∞ ∞

Through long and steady effort, the senior bureaucrat reaches his goal. But his satisfaction is short-lived since, by then, retirement is close at hand.

The senior bureaucrat passes over and rejects as obscure and unintelligible those things he does not understand. This mental limit of his becomes a standard that his subordinates are compelled to observe. In other words, not transcend.

∞ ∞ ∞

When he is depressed, the senior bureaucrat laments his many vile defects. But, magnanimous and merciful, he always forgives himself in the end.

∞ ∞ ∞

Senior public servants have no reason to emulate oysters. Except, perhaps, for their shells.

∞ ∞ ∞

A member of the mandarinate is a vaudeville ditty rather than a symphony, house wine rather than champagne, sweetener rather than sugar, vinyl instead of leather, glass and not crystal, tin and not steel. Get the picture?

∞ ∞ ∞

For the senior bureaucrat, it is more important to be heard than to listen. Which is why he excels in the art of speaking, and has never mastered the art of silence.

∞ ∞ ∞

We might be tempted to interpret the mandarin's determination, conviction and status as intelligence, depth and logic. Discernment is needed to realize that when the powerful fool makes mistakes, he does so triumphantly. So triumphantly that his errors become contagious, and tend to create agreement without judgement's prior consent.

∞ ∞ ∞

When a senior public servant makes a decision, there is more will than intelligence in it.

∞ ∞ ∞

The senior bureaucrat: a well-balanced combination of ambition, self-confidence and incompetence.

∞ ∞ ∞

Doubt, which in most people is part of a healthy outlook on life, becomes for the senior bureaucrat a sign of weakness, wavering and lack of decision.

∞ ∞ ∞

The senior bureaucrat thinks badly when he thinks at all, but his calm, self-assured voice compensates and persuades. Illusion triumphs.

∞ ∞ ∞

Among the mandarinate, plain common sense has a way of dressing itself up in vestments of wisdom and profundity.

∞ ∞ ∞

A senior public servant's sense of motivation is like a fragile, flickering flame that the slightest setback threatens as if it were a squall. Encouragement makes it shoot up and spark like a bonfire, but it diminishes, shrinks, suffocates, then gutters out into warm wax as soon as the attention and regard of other people is lacking.

∞ ∞ ∞

Those senior bureaucrats who are not myopic tend to be long-sighted.

∞ ∞ ∞

To achieve take-off, the senior bureaucrat's mind requires a strong headwind. A drawback due not so much to overloading as to problems in the basic design.

∞ ∞ ∞

Words in the mandarin's mouth are usually simple and fac-ile. The thoughts they must transmit are not.

∞ ∞ ∞

Unfortunately, senior bureaucrats preserve the traits of their youth into maturity and beyond to old age, where they strike a jarring note. Like the picture of an old man with a soprano voice and short pants.

∞ ∞ ∞

When this senior bureaucrat makes a play on words, he is the first to be surprised. Then he excuses himself as if something accidental and involuntary had slipped out.

∞ ∞ ∞

The quality of a mind is measured more by the nature and rightness of the questions asked than by the precision and rel-evance of the answers offered. The question establishes the tone and level of the conversation, whereas the answer, being sec-ondary, rarely escapes the question's weight and gravity. The senior bureaucrat asks very few questions, either of himself, or of other people. But he'll give as many answers as necessary.

∞ ∞ ∞

There is little latitude for laughter in the highly studied dig-nity of the mandarin. The fragile structure of the latter can hardly survive the frank brutality of the former.

∞ ∞ ∞

When he reflects, the senior bureaucrat often emits sounds under his breath, a kind of grave and personal rumbling. These guide him through the labyrinth of his thoughts, the way the cries of a bat help it avoid obstacles and steer it toward open air.

∞ ∞ ∞

In the senior Public Service, broadness of spirit often has a narrow neck.

∞ ∞ ∞

Everything depends on the choice that is made. If the senior bureaucrat makes the right decision, what follows is easy and unfolds according to plan. If he chooses badly, he will apply all his energy defending his pride and ego and will stubbornly refuse to rethink his point of view, or change his mind, or admit his error and go back on his decision. Infallibility is a temptation difficult to resist.

∞ ∞ ∞

Every senior public servant is in full mastery of the quality Napoleon thought essential for a powerful and victorious army: the ability to offer maximum resistance at all times.

∞ ∞ ∞

In order to remember something, the mandarin must first forget it several times.

∞ ∞ ∞

An idea is to the mind of the mandarin what his gestures are to his body. There is a direct correlation, a conformity, between them. This is perfectly fitting and perfectly depressing.

∞ ∞ ∞

Many people live their entire lives without letting on that they think little or not at all. Among the mandarinate, it shows.

∞ ∞ ∞

The senior bureaucrat rebels against the laws of nature, which had decided he was to be mediocre, by fighting tooth and nail against the decision. A vain struggle: he remains mediocre. But his courage and perseverance are very touching.

∞ ∞ ∞

If the senior bureaucrat could acquire all of the qualities he wants to have, he would gladly do without any virtue at all.

∞ ∞ ∞

The senior public servant who momentarily strays down unknown intellectual paths is sometimes frightened by his brain's possibilities. He hurries back to find security in routine, the way a fearful child scurries back to a lighted room.

∞ ∞ ∞

Like certain French wines that do not travel and must be drunk in the vineyard, the thoughts of the mandarin are luminous or seem so only in the bureaucratic environment where they were born and grew. Take them out of their setting, transport them, export them elsewhere, and they fizzle out and die. They are like diaphanous seaweed, ruffled, drifting, graceful forms as they float, but which droop into an amorphous mass if you take them out of the water.

20
Knowledge

In the senior Public Service, reading and sleeping share a common, but unclear, boundary.

∞ ∞ ∞

The senior bureaucrat possesses a deep knowledge of very complex things which have absolutely no importance.

∞ ∞ ∞

The mandarin considers a university degree important when it comes to selecting candidates for an upper-echelon position, less as a means of measuring how well they will fill the bill, than as a way of finding an easy and convenient pretext to exclude one of them from the competition. "Your degree is not in the discipline we are looking for," he will say. In fact, he is more willing to accept candidates who have no degree at all — as is often his own case — than those who have one or several in another discipline. You see, in his eyes, ignorance is the guarantor of innocence, malleability, a certain submissiveness, while knowledge, whatever its nature, can quickly turn into a threatening expression of protest and defiance.

∞ ∞ ∞

Asked what degrees he himself has, the senior public servant tends to grow vague and evasive, and directs your attention to the passing clouds.

∞ ∞ ∞

Though the senior bureaucrat is always glad to serve on a selection committee, something bothers him. He knows that if he had to undergo the same scrutiny, he would certainly fail . . . But he thanks his lucky stars that his role is to ask questions, not give answers. Each to his speciality, after all.

∞ ∞ ∞

Like the cuckold, the senior public servant is always the last to know about what should concern him most, and what the rest of the world already knows.

∞ ∞ ∞

A senior bureaucrat is often a very ordinary, even mediocre, person. But force of circumstance has provided him with a first-rate education, possibly at an institution of great renown. The years have passed. Today, he presents the compelling spectacle of his being and his knowledge tugging and pulling at each other, the latter winning out over the former.

∞ ∞ ∞

The kingdom of senior bureaucrats is teeming with individuals who never finished their studies, from lack of courage, or never earned the coveted degree, for lack of talent. If this is not your case, you would do well to hide your science, suppress your high-sounding titles and bury your golden certificates. Because you are not like them, the mandarinate will discard you, ban you, ostracize you. True knowledge, as they will tell you, is not learned in school — a dangerous mirage — but resides in experience, which itself demands no particular virtue except longevity. Besides, degrees create intellectuals, philosophers and similar thinkers, all individualistic, undesirable and dangerous types who have no real sense of the way things work.

Then again, there are always some senior bureaucrats who will tell you in confidence that the first criterion for merit — speaking unofficially of course, off the record — is not to have a degree. Except, of course, those people in specialized positions who pass their lives in one particular cubby-hole, slaves who do nothing but provide data, statistics, arguments and briefing notes for their superiors, the mandarin class with few or no degrees.

"If I were forced by circumstances to leave the Public Service," a mandarin confided to me once, "I would starve to death. Being a senior bureaucrat is all I can do in life."

∞ ∞ ∞

Among great minds, doubt is born of knowledge. Among the mandarinate, certainty is born of ignorance.

∞ ∞ ∞

The senior public servant is terrified by words. He won't undertake to read *The Oxford Nursery Rhyme Book* without the *Oxford English Dictionary* open at his side.

∞ ∞ ∞

The senior bureaucrat really has to admit it this time — after all, hasn't his assistant told him that more than once? — he had a stroke of pure genius . . . . What inspiration! That memo he just signed was a real masterpiece, stating that from now on he would read no document longer than one page, no matter who wrote it or what the subject was. It made a big splash, stressing conciseness, moderation, greater efficiency, rigour of thought, economy of time and energy . . . As well, those endless documents sent to him from his various services ate up enormous time and demanded an excessive amount of concentration. Imagine the difficulty of reading all of those words, one after the other, without stopping, without rest. Not only that, you had to try to understand them, too, at the same time you were reading them! That's close to mental cruelty. Yes, it was time to put a stop to all that. Hence, the memo . . . Not that the senior public servant despises writing, but he prefers action, which is less demanding, less exhausting. Or else oral expression, an area in which he excels . . .

∞ ∞ ∞

If you are bawling out a senior bureaucrat, never use difficult words. You will put him in the awkward situation of not being able to react immediately, or reacting only with hazy and evasive answers. Until he has had a chance to consult his dictionary.

∞ ∞ ∞

Ignorance looks good in a member of the mandarinate. There is something natural, suitable, legitimate about it. It's the normal way of things. His knowledge, he seems to be telling us, is elsewhere. But where?

∞ ∞ ∞

When he cannot understand a difficult concept, the mandarin cries, "Mere philosophy!" In other words, unreal, abstract, impractical. For him, reality stops and coincides with the borders of his understanding. A prisoner of his own circle, he cannot picture a larger circle that others can imagine or understand.

∞ ∞ ∞

The sum of a senior bureaucrat's knowledge fits into the wafer-thin leather case wedged under his arm. The bulging briefcase in his hand is for the wisdom of others.

∞ ∞ ∞

There is something sad about the jolly mood of mandarins together at a party. That which escapes them is so obvious, so enormous, so menacing that it should be enough, we think, to strike their imaginations, to create a healthy anxiety in them and administer a bracing shock. But instead, they amuse themselves, unconcerned by what they do not see, happy in their ignorance. Just as, on the parlour rug, beneath a midnight moon, a frisky young mouse gambols under the transfixed eye of the cat who is ready to pounce.

∞ ∞ ∞

The senior bureaucrat reminds the candidate that he did not finish his studies at university. However — and here he is as sincere as can be — it doesn't occur to him that he did not get his degree either, nor did he even study the subject at hand. How can he do this? Through the habit of seeing himself as a being above all others, to whom the usual rules governing humankind do not apply.

∞ ∞ ∞

The senior bureaucrat is content with his lot, and is never tempted to push back the border marking the end of his knowledge.

∞ ∞ ∞

Dictionaries and the senior bureaucrat rarely see eye to eye, with the former often contradicting the latter. It's no wonder those heavy volumes are cast aside and sit gathering dust on a shelf . . . Fortunately, grammar is less sticky and lends itself better to the liberties that senior public servants take with it.

∞ ∞ ∞

That which the senior bureaucrat does not know, he prefers not to know. Even when he knows, he does not care to, knowing it is not important to know.

∞ ∞ ∞

Perhaps the vocabulary of the senior public servant, so specialized and restricted, is to blame for holding down his spirit; perhaps, with a different language, he would have reached a higher plane.

∞ ∞ ∞

The words in the mandarin's vocabulary inhabit a fuzzy zone of ambiguity, and this contagion spills over into his thought. Therein, perhaps, is the reason for that staggering, searching quality he has.

∞ ∞ ∞

At times there are problems that the senior public servant understands only vaguely, and is unable to write about. Fortunately, he can always discuss them with loquacity and aplomb.

∞ ∞ ∞

Whether speaking or writing, the senior bureaucrat always presents his words in bulk.

∞ ∞ ∞

The discovery of injustice and the potential it holds is as important in the life of a mandarin as walking is in a child's young existence, or as the shuddering joys of a first orgasm. It is as if doors that, up until then, had been closed were opening wide, doors which had remained shut or ajar much too long because of his outdated Christian morality. Suddenly, his range of possibilities grows in huge proportion, and new freedom is offered him, as he represses, then leaves behind, rules and familiar limits. His goals multiply, as do the means to reach them. Injustice increases the senior bureaucrat's power and will in the same way that, in the world of computers and software, we can double our storage and information processing potential simply by using a double-sided disk.

∞ ∞ ∞

Why does learning, whatever kind it is, seem so arduous to the senior public servant? Because he must fight the ingrained habit of holding on to what he already knows.

∞ ∞ ∞

Conciseness is not his strength, for it demands superior intelligence, teamed with a will to intensify and concentrate an idea. It demands a certain skill and aptitude in the balancing of abstract concepts without excessive effort. Otherwise, the process would drain away the energy required for the idea itself. And it demands that we make minimal use of the inefficient and heavy-handed agent called language, and use words like markers to help us find our way in unknown territory, rather than as closed containers literally transporting the substance of the idea . . . The thought remains fluid, floating free and going where it wishes, in constant innovation like a device in perpetual self-creation, in continual generation.

The thoughts of a senior bureaucrat, on the other hand, scatter in all directions, like spilled alcohol, like liquid oxygen, like a drop of mercury pressed under the finger. When he seeks to put his thought on paper in hopes of pinning it down, identifying it, locating it, it suddenly begins to resemble dictation misheard, it totters under tons of useless words, repetition, circumlocution. It is diluted, it drowns in speech. It is there, surely, but in such feeble concentration that there is little hope of distilling any meaning or profit from it, just as we must give up on the dream of gathering the abundant gold suspended in sea water.

∞ ∞ ∞

The problem in my job, says the senior bureaucrat, is that it's impossible to know anything perfectly, or ignore anything completely. On one hand, I can't compete with a colleague, nor even with an underling, who has a specialization in a given area. Yet I can hardly plead ignorance, since bits of information always reach my ears, and I can't deny that without being accused of lying. What a curse it is to know only a little! How frightening it is to forever be leaping into the void! And we must make decisions on the shakiest of grounds, without ever showing a hint of our difficulty, our uncertainty.

Dear God, deliver me from my scruples, so I may be just like the other mandarins.